BROOKLANDS BOOKS

CHEVROLET
1955-1957

Compiled by
R.M. Clarke

ISBN 1 869826 787

Distributed by
Brooklands Book Distribution Ltd.
'Holmerise', Seven Hills Road,
Cobham, Surrey, England

BROOKLANDS BOOKS SERIES

AC Ace & Aceca 1953-1983
AC Cobra 1962-1969
Alfa Romeo Giulia Berlinas 1962-1976
Alfa Romeo Giulia Coupés 1963-1976
Alfa Romeo Spider 1966-1987
Aston Martin Gold Portfolio 1972-1985
Austin Seven 1922-1982
Austin A30 & A35 1951-1962
Austin Healey 100 1952-1959
Austin Healey 3000 1959 1967
Austin Healey 100 & 3000 Collection No. 1
Austin Healey 'Frogeye' Sprite Collection No. 1
Austin Healey Sprite 1958-1971
Avanti 1962-1983
BMW Six Cylinder Coupés 1969-1975
BMW 1600 Collection No. 1
BMW 2002 1968-1976
Bristol Cars Gold Portfolio 1946-1985
Buick Riviera 1963-1978
Cadillac Automobiles 1949-1959
Cadillac Eldorado 1967 1978
Cadillac in the Sixties No. 1
Camaro 1966-1970
Chevrolet 1955-1957
Chevrolet Camaro Collection No. 1
Chevelle & SS 1964-1972
Chevy II Nova & SS 1962-1973
Chrysler 300 1955-1970
Citroen Traction Avant 1934-1957
Citroen 2CV 1949-1982
Cobras & Replicas 1962-1983
Cortina 1600E & GT 1967-1970
Corvair 1959 1968
Daimler Dart & V-8 250 1959-1969
Datsun 240z & 260z 1970-1977
De Tomaso Collection No. 1
Dodge Charger 1966-1974
Excalibur Collection No. 1
Ferrari Cars 1946-1956
Ferrari Cars 1962-1966
Ferrari Cars 1969-1973
Ferrari Dino 1965-1974
Ferrari Dino 308 1974 1979
Ferrari 308 & Mondial 1980-1984
Ferrari Collection No. 1
Fiat X1/9 1972 1980
Ford Falcon 1960-1970
Ford Mustang 1964-1967
Ford Mustang 1967-1973
Ford RS Escort 1968 1980
High Performance Escorts MkI 1968-1974
High Performance Escorts MkII 1975-1980
Hudson & Railton Cars 1936-1940
Jaguar (& S.S) Cars 1931-1937
Jaguar Cars 1957-1961
Jaguar Cars 1961-1964
Jaguar Cars 1964-1968
Jaguar E-Type 1961-1966
Jaguar E Type 1966-1971
Jaguar XKE Collection No. 1
Jaguar XJ6 1968-1972
Jaguar XJ6 Series II 1973-1979
Jaguar XJ6 & XJ12 Series III 1979-1985
Jaguar XJ12 1972 1980
Jaguar XJS 1975-1980
Jensen Cars 1946-1967
Jensen Cars 1967-1979
Jensen Interceptor Gold Portfolio 1966-1986
Lamborghini Cars 1964-1970
Lamborghini Cars 1970-1975
Lamborghini Countach Collection No. 1
Lamborghini Countach & Urraco 1974-1980
Lamborghini Countach & Jalpa 1980-1985
Lancia Stratos 1972 1985
Land Rover 1948-1973
Land Rover Series II & IIa 1958-1971
Land Rover Series III 1971-1985
Lotus Cortina 1963-1970
Lotus Elan 1962-1973
Lotus Elan Collection No. 1
Lotus Elan Collection No. 2
Lotus Elite 1957-1964
Lotus Elite & Eclat 1974-1981
Lotus Turbo Esprit 1980-1986
Lotus Europa 1966-1975
Lotus Europa Collection No. 1
Lotus Seven 1957-1980
Lotus Seven Collection No. 1
Maserati 1965-1970
Maserati 1970-1975
Mazda RX-7 Collection No. 1
Mercedes 230/250/280SL 1963-1971
Mercedes 350/450SL & SLC 1971-1980
Mercedes Benz Cars 1949-1954
Mercedes Benz Cars 1954-1957
Mercedes Benz Cars 1957-1961
Mercedes Benz Competition Cars 1950-1957
Metropolitan 1954-1962
MG Cars 1929-1934
MG TC 1945-1949
MG TD 1949-1953
MG TF 1953-1955

MG Cars 1957 1959
MG Cars 1959-1962
MG Midget 1961-1980
MG MGA 1955-1962
MGA Collection No. 1
MGB Roadsters 1962-1980
MGB GT 1965-1980
Mini Cooper 1961-1971
Morgan Cars 1960-1970
Morgan Cars 1969-1979
Morris Minor Collection No. 1
Old's Cutlass & 4-4-2 1964-1972
Oldsmobile Toronado 1966-1978
Opel GT 1968-1973
Pantera 1970-1973
Pantera & Mangusta 1969-1974
Plymouth Barracuda 1964-1974
Pontiac GTO 1964 1970
Pontiac Firebird 1967-1973
Pontiac Tempest & GTO 1961-1965
Porsche Cars 1960-1964
Porsche Cars 1964-1968
Porsche Cars 1968-1972
Porsche Cars in the Sixties
Porsche Cars 1972-1975
Porsche 356 1952-1965
Porsche 911 Collection No. 1
Porsche 911 Collection No. 2
Porsche 911 1965-1969
Porsche 911 1970-1972
Porsche 911 1973-1977
Porsche 911 Carrera 1973-1977
Porsche 911 SC 1978-1983
Porsche 911 Turbo 1975-1984
Porsche 914 1969-1975
Porsche 914 Collection No. 1
Porsche 924 1975-1981
Porsche 928 Collection No. 1
Porsche 944 1981-1985
Porsche Turbo Collection No. 1
Reliant Scimitar 1964-1986
Rolls Royce Silver Cloud 1955-1965
Rolls Royce Silver Shadow 1965-1980
Range Rover 1970-1981
Rover 3 & 3.5 Litre 1958-1973
Rover P4 1949-1959
Rover P4 1955-1964
Rover 2000 + 2200 1963-1977
Rover 3500 1968-1977
Rover 3500 & Vitesse 1976-1986
Saab Sonett Collection No. 1
Saab Turbo 1976-1983
Singer Sports Cars 1933-1934
Studebaker Hawks & Larks 1956-1963
Sunbeam Alpine & Tiger 1959-1967
Thunderbird 1955 1957
Thunderbird 1958-1963
Triumph 2000-2.5-2500 1963-1977
Triumph Spitfire 1962-1980
Triumph Spitfire Collection No. 1
Triumph Stag 1970-1980
Triumph Stag Collection No. 1
Triumph TR2 & TR3 1952 1960
Triumph TR4.TR5.TR250 1961-1968
Triumph TR6 1969-1976
Triumph TR6 Collection No. 1
Triumph TR7 & TR8 1975-1981
Triumph GT6 1966-1974
Triumph Vitesse & Herald 1959 1971
TVR 1960-1980
Volkswagen Cars 1936-1956
VW Beetle 1956-1977
VW Beetle Collection No. 1
VW Golf GTi 1976-1986
VW Karmann Ghia 1955-1982
VW Scirocco 1974-1981
Volvo 1800 1960-1973
Volvo 120 Series 1956-1970

BROOKLANDS MUSCLE CARS SERIES
American Motors Muscle Cars 1966-1970
Buick Muscle Cars 1965-1970
Camaro Muscle Cars 1966-1972
Capri Muscle Cars 1969-1983
Chevrolet Muscle Cars 1966-1972
Dodge Muscle Cars 1967-1970
Mercury Muscle Cars 1966-1971
Mini Muscle Cars 1961-1979
Mopar Muscle Cars 1964-1967
Mopar Muscle Cars 1968-1971
Mustang Muscle Cars 1967-1971
Shelby Mustang Muscle Cars 1965-1970
Oldsmobile Muscle Cars 1964-1970
Plymouth Muscle Cars 1966-1971
Pontiac Muscle Cars 1966-1972
Muscle Cars Compared 1966-1971
Muscle Cars Compared Book 2 1965-1971

BROOKLANDS ROAD & TRACK SERIES
Road & Track on Alfa Romeo 1949-1963
Road & Track on Alfa Romeo 1964-1970
Road & Track on Alfa Romeo 1971-1976
Road & Track on Alfa Romeo 1977 1984
Road & Track on Aston Martin 1962-1984

Road & Track on Audi 1952-1980
Road & Track on Audi 1980-1986
Road & Track on Austin Healey 1953-1970
Road & Track on BMW Cars 1966-1974
Road & Track on BMW Cars 1975-1978
Road & Track on BMW Cars 1979-1983
Road & Track on Cobra, Shelby &
   Ford GT40 1962-1983
Road & Track on Corvette 1953-1967
Road & Track on Corvette 1968-1982
Road & Track on Corvette 1982-1986
Road & Track on Datsun Z 1970-1983
Road & Track on Ferrari 1950-1968
Road & Track on Ferrari 1968-1974
Road & Track on Ferrari 1975-1981
Road & Track on Ferrari 1981-1984
Road & Track on Fiat Sports Cars 1968-1981
Road & Track on Jaguar 1950-1960
Road & Track on Jaguar 1961 1968
Road & Track on Jaguar 1968-1974
Road & Track on Jaguar 1974-1982
Road & Track on Lamborghini 1964-1985
Road & Track on Lotus 1972-1981
Road & Track on Maserati 1952-1974
Road & Track on Maserati 1975-1983
Road & Track on Mazda RX7 1978-1986
Road & Track on Mercedes Sports & GT Cars
   1970-1980
Road & Track on MG Sports Cars 1949-1961
Road & Track on MG Sports Cars 1962 1980
Road & Track on Mustang 1964-1977
Road & Track on Peugeot 1955 1986
Road & Track on Pontiac 1960 1983
Road & Track on Porsche 1951 1967
Road & Track on Porsche 1968-1971
Road & Track on Porsche 1972-1975
Road & Track on Porsche 1975 1978
Road & Track on Porsche 1979-1982
Road & Track on Porsche 1982-1985
Road & Track on Rolls Royce & Bentley 1950-1965
Road & Track on Rolls Royce & Bentley 1966-1984
Road & Track on Saab 1955-1985
Road & Track on Toyota Sports & G T Cars 1966-1986
Road & Track on Triumph Sports Cars 1953-1967
Road & Track on Triumph Sports Cars 1967-1974
Road & Track on Triumph Sports Cars 1974-1982
Road & Track on Volkswagen 1951 1968
Road & Track on Volkswagen 1968 1978
Road & Track on Volkswagen 1978-1985
Road & Track on Volvo 1957-1974
Road & Track on Volvo 1975-1985

BROOKLANDS CAR AND DRIVER SERIES
Car and Driver on BMW 1955-1977
Car and Driver on BMW 1977-1985
Car and Driver on Cobra, Shelby & Ford GT40
   1963-1984
Car and Driver on Datsun Z 1600 & 2000
   1966-1984
Car and Driver on Corvette 1956-1967
Car and Driver on Corvette 1968 1977
Car and Driver on Corvette 1978-1982
Car and Driver on Ferrari 1955-1962
Car and Driver on Ferrari 1963-1975
Car and Driver on Ferrari 1976-1983
Car and Driver on Mopar 1956-1967
Car and Driver on Mopar 1968 1975
Car and Driver on Pontiac 1961-1975
Car and Driver on Porsche 1955 1962
Car and Driver on Porsche 1963-1970
Car and Driver on Porsche 1970-1976
Car and Driver on Porsche 1977-1981
Car and Driver on Porsche 1982 1986
Car and Driver on Saab 1956-1985
Car and Driver on Volvo 1955-1986

BROOKLANDS MOTOR & THOROUGHBRED & CLASSIC CAR SERIES
Motor & T & CC on Ferrari 1966-1976
Motor & T & CC on Ferrari 1976-1984
Motor & T & CC on Lotus 1979 1983
Motor & T & CC on Morris Minor 1948-1983

BROOKLANDS PRACTICAL CLASSICS SERIES
Practical Classics on MGB Restoration
Practical Classics on Midget/Sprite Restoration
Practical Classics on Mini Cooper Restoration
Practical Classics on Morris Minor Restoration
Practical Classics on Landrover Restoration
Practical Classics on V W Beele Restoration

BROOKLANDS MILITARY VEHICLES SERIES
Allied Military Vehicles Collection No. 1
Allied Military Vehicles Collection No. 2
Dodge Military Vehicles Collection No. 1
Military Jeeps 1941-1945
Off Road Jeeps 1944-1971
V W Kugelwagen 1940-1975

BROOKLANDS BOOKS

CONTENTS

BROOKLANDS BOOKS

ACKNOWLEDGEMENTS

We recently conducted a survey of our customers and were gratified to find that half of the current sales of our books are bought by people who already own one of our earlier titles. If you fall into this category I would suggest that you pay no further heed to this introduction and turn immediately to page 86 and digest what that informed writer, Jay Storer, has to say about the 'Good Old '55 to 57s'.

For those who have not come upon a Brooklands publication before, I should warn you that you will find nothing within these covers that is original. Our function for over 20 years has been to act as an archival service for today's owners of interesting automobiles by making available to them road tests and other technical pieces that were written about their vehicles when they were new. It is hoped that by re-issuing these stories it will help enthusiasts to understand how their cars have gained 'collectible' status and make the task of historians, who thirst for this hard to locate information, that much easier.

Although we can take some credit for organising and producing the books in this series, which now number over 200, readers should understand that their gratitude should really be directed to the enlightened publishers and authors of the original material, who generously allow us to reprint their copyright articles. In this instance we are indebted to the management of Auto Age, Car Life, Modern Motor, Motor Life, Motor Trend, Petersens Publications, Road & Track, Speed Age, and Wheels for their help and on-going support.

R.M. Clarke

Lines of the lowered bodies give Chevrolet for 1955 an appearance of motion even when the cars are parked. Shown here is the Bel Air 4-door sedan, one of 14 models incorporating chassis improvements.

Chevrolet

The Bel Air sport coupe is an example of Chevrolet's "profile styling." The dip in the belt line and the horizontal planes of the fenders and chrome mouldings are interesting with two-tone combinations.

The new Chevrolets offer a V-8 engine for the first time in 35 years. The entire line of 14 models has a lower, fleeter silhouette with redesigned frames for more passenger room.

1955 CHEVROLET MODELS

210 Series

2-door Sedan
4-door Sedan
2-door Station Wagon
4-door Station Wagon
Club Coupe

150 Series

2-door Sedan
4-door Sedan
2-door Station Wagon
Utility Sedan

Bel Air Series

2-door Sedan
4-door Sedan
4-door Station Wagon
Sport Coupe
Convertible

PRONOUNCED mechanical advances plus new riding comfort and a complete re-styling of bodies give Chevrolet for 1955 its most spectacular model announcement.

No major part of the car has been overlooked in the broadscale improvement program. Driving ease and riding comfort benefit along with the creation of fresh automotive design. The accomplishment, says the company, has been possible only because of a thorough job of product re-engineering and the tremendous new plant facilities Chevrolet adds this year. From an extraordinary long list of new features, these are particularly outstanding:

1—First automobiles in the low-price field to reflect the "dream car" influence of the General Motors Motoramas. All roofs have been visibly lowered with a corresponding reduction in hood and belt lines to accentuate a longer, fleeter appearance. Overall, sedans have been lowered two and one-half inches, station wagons as much as six. At the same time, passenger room has been increased.

2—First V8 engine offered on a Chevrolet in 35 years. Profiting by recent research in combustion and manufacturing techniques, the V8 is unveiled as "far more precisely built and efficient in performance than others in its class." Named the "Turbo-Fire V8," the V8 delivers 162 horsepower.

3—Higher horsepower ratings and new quietness and smoothness in two "Blue Flame" sixes. Engines are of the traditional valve-in-head design, which in the last few years has won virtually 100 percent acceptance. A 123-horsepower engine is available with the manual gearshift. The six built exclusively for the Powerglide automatic transmission now develops 136 horsepower.

4—Integrated body and frame design. Chevrolet points out it has been able to obtain close unity with body and frame by engineering components to complement each other. An important reduction in vibration has been effected and weight saved. The frame is more rectangular and twist-resistant. With a scientific repositioning of mounts and the utmost application of rubber insulation, the body is isolated from road shocks to an unusual degree.

5—Front and rear suspensions revamped. Added riding comfort and roadability, Chevrolet states, are assured by vastly improved suspensions. At the front, a modern version of the ball-joint design aids car handling and steering as well as comfort. One improvement

First low-priced General Motors car to reflect the "dream" influence, the convertible has real dash. New styling is carried through to the rear bumper with trunk deck and tail lamps enhancing appearance.

Six cylinder engines and chassis are shown below. Prominent advances over previous power plans are the rugged frame members, side-mounted air cleaner, Hotchkiss drive and outrigger rear suspension. Frames are lighter for '55.

new to the industry is a control arm geometry that cancels out most of the objectionable "dive" that often accompanies brake stops. The suspension also applies a new and more durable lightweight bearing material while the design decreases lubrication points from 16 to 4. Rear suspension improvements include leaf springs nine inches longer to an overall length of 58 inches. For stability, rear spring mounts are outside the frame, after the fashion of the Chevrolet Corvette.

6—Increased safety through greater visibility. Every car window of safety plate glass—front, rear and side—is larger in 1955 Chevrolet bodies. The gain is due largely to the extension of glass over areas that have been "blind spots" since the early days of the automobile. Increase in visibility through the sweepsight windshield alone is 19 per cent. As another example of the improvement, glass area in four-door sedans totals 24.5 square feet.

7—Optional overdrive. An overdrive installation will be offered for the first time. Engine speed reduction of more than 20 percent is accomplished by the overdrive which automatically cuts in when the foot is lifted off the accelerator about 31 miles an hour. Operating economy is better while reduced engine revolutions also give smoother, quieter performance. Less clutch operation in city driving is still another advantage. Optional overdrive brings to six the number of "power packages" available on each of 14 Chevrolet passenger car models.

8—More electrical power. A 12-volt electrical system will furnish ample reserve power for the ever-growing demands of accessories. The system is standard on both sixes and V8s, assuring increased generator efficiency and higher starting motor speeds. Another safety feature is a dual circuit breaker. A short circuit or overload will, as a consequence, not entirely disable the system.

9—"Dry Air" ventilation. This feature involves an arch-shaped plenum chamber that channels fresh air from a slotted cowl vent. Drainage from the chamber prevents any water from reaching passengers, even in rainiest weather. Cowl-installed and extended to the frame on each side, the plenum chamber acts as a structural brace as well. In addition, it is a perfect adjunct to an all-weather air conditioner which Chevrolet introduces this year as optional equipment.

10—Tubeless tires for increased safety. The casing remains the same, but instead of an inner tube, interior surfaces are coated with a butyl "skin" for sealing. Blowouts are resisted and deflation slower with punctures.

11—Smoother power application. The torque tube drive is replaced by a Hotchkiss drive to deliver power more smoothly to the rear wheels and to provide a "flatter" ride in combination with the longer springs. According to engineers, the "work-out" of a new axle, springs and drive line, together with new engine mounts achieve a velvet-like transmission of power.

12—Easier steering. From power steering, an improved version of which is available on 1955 cars, Chevrolet has adopted the recirculating ball-nut gear and combined it with a relay type of linkage that increases smoothness and reduces driver effort. A more rigid wheel coupling and truer geometry is also claimed.

Changes in Body Design

Most distinguishing mark of the new Chevrolet bodies is their low-slung silhouettes and vertical windshield pillars. Broad, flat hood and trunk lids are approximately three and one-half inches lower than last year, while the high, straight crown of the fenders enhances an impression of fleetness and agility. The design gives the cars the appearance of much greater length although wheelbases remain unchanged.

Brand new among 14 bodies on the 150, 210 and Bel Air series are two-door station wagons. The complete line-up shows two- and four-door sedans in all series, two-door station wagons in the 150 and 210, four-door station wagons in the 210 and Bel Air, a utility sedan in the 150, a club coupe in the 210 and sport and convertible coupes in the Bel Air series.

Even more appealing colors than the brilliant array of 1954 are available. Of 14 solid color options, ten are new. All 21 of the two-tone paint combinations are new except one. An interesting sidelight is a special two-toning option on Bel Air convertibles and sport coupes which extends the top color onto

The station wagon is gaining popularity and the Bel Air Beauville, Chevrolet says, promises to create ultra-new standards for styling beauty in two new series of models.

the rear deck and quarter panels. Unusually luxurious interiors combine harmonizing colors and a variety of cloths and plastics.

More Compact Engine

A result of years of research and hundreds of thousands of miles of severe testing, the valve-in-head V8 carries a compression ratio of 8 to 1 and a displacement of 265 cubic inches. The engine is exceedingly compact with a bore of 3.75 and a stroke of 3 inches. The stroke is the shortest in the industry, a factor which signifies less piston travel per mile and great smoothness.

Although Chevrolet has had V8s under experiment since it tried out this design in 1917-19, the "Turbo-Fire V8" entails basic re-design in the last three years. Engineers sought the compactness of a short crankshaft with the power of large displacement.

The bore is said to be unusually large for an engine of the "Turbo-Fire V8's" length. The combustion chamber is wedge-shaped to provide virtual total combustion of fuel fed by double-throated carburetor. With a minimum of friction and high thermal efficiency, the economy of operation is said to be exceptional.

Manufacturing processes complement the compact design to assure unusually fine balance of working parts. Not only is the crankshaft balanced on a newly developed machine with electronically controlled indicators, but a final balance is achieved after assembly. The last balance test takes place before installation of the oil pan.

The brake and clutch pedals are 'hung' from the dashboard panel this year, red warning lights take the place of ammeter and oil gauge, and glove compartment is centered. Overdrive is an optional.

In the case of the sixes it was necessary to design a side-mounted air cleaner and re-position the fan in order to obtain the low silhouette dictated by decreased hood heights. Simultaneously, added efficiency and quietness have been credited to modifications which include a re-designed water pump, larger fan and a completely new fuel pump that guarantees more constant fuel pressures.

Frame is Stiffer

The 1955 Chevrolet frame has 50 percent greater resistance to twisting although 18 percent lighter. This has been brought about by stiffer frame side members, a rearrangement of side members and a more strategic placement of engine and body mounts. Side members are 14.5 inches farther apart at the narrowest point and four inches closer together at the rear. Straightening of side members has reduced twisting tendencies created by vertical loads.

Before determining the location of the new engine mounts, Chevrolet ran exhaustive tests to fix the areas of least vibration. They then established the mountings as close to these areas as practical.

The four-point mounts that supplant the three-point mounts of 1954 models were devised so as not to interfere with the natural balance of the engines, and at the same time prevent uneven distribution of torque reactions.

Front mounts are strut-type and attached to brackets on each side of the cylinder block at the lower corners and angle to seats on the frame front cross member. The rear mounts are located between the lower rear edges of the clutch housing and short brackets cantilevered from the frame side members.

Rubber insulation is introduced both front and rear. Front mountings make use of biscuit-size rubber pads mounted on a spacing tube. These layers of insulation are both above and below the brackets and frame cross member. The pads between rear brackets and frame side members act in shear during engine roll and essentially in shear for engine support.

A compact, 162 hp V-8 powerhouse, the new 'Turbo-Fire' Chevrolet engine has 265 cu. in. displacement and compression ratio of 8 to 1. It still maintains the traditional valve-in-head.

Transmission is Improved

New three-speed transmissions have more load-carrying capacity and structural durability. The gearshift mechanism has been improved. Previously the shaft was mounted along the steering column. For 1955 the shaft is enclosed within the column, producing a "cleaner" appearance.

The overdrive unit available on three-speed transmissions may be locked out if desired. It involves the substitution of the 3.7:1 ratio rear axle with a high performance 4.11:1 axle in addition to the overdrive mechanism. Chevrolet reports the overdrive reduces engine speed by 22 percent, amounting to 615 fewer revolutions per mile. This can represent considerable saving in gas and oil consumption.

Most significant improvement in the Powerglide automatic transmission has been the development of a new low range band of unique, double-wrap design. Downshifts are softer and upshifts smoother. The selector lever is concentric with the steering column and, as an assistance to those unfamiliar with Powerglide, an illuminated quadrant on the instrument panel tells the position of the selector.

Ammeter and oil pressure gauges have been dropped from the instrument panel and red warning lights substituted. The glove compartment is now in the center of the panel for the greater convenience of drivers. Another among scores of improvements is the perfect counterbalance of trunk lids and hoods. With this feature, they will remain open at any angle. Another innovation is the angled mechanism which will permit full lowering of rear windows on two-door sedans.

Relocation of parts in power steering mechanisms from the engine compartment to the steering linkage has improved serviceability. This thought was also in mind when the master brake cylinder was placed under the hood. The brake pedal, suspended this year, gets nylon bushings to eliminate the need for lubrication. Power brakes are optional.

The rear axle has greater torque capacity and better oil sealing. Area of the clutch disc has been enlarged one-fifth to provide increased durability.

Many "Optionals"

Chevrolet's all-weather air conditioner will be available only with V8s as an option. Mechanism for this impressive comfort feature is located underneath the hood and instrument panel, leaving the luggage compartment clear. Nozzles to expel cool air into the passenger compartment are at ends of the instrument panel.

Hooded headlights, inward slope of radiator grille and a newly designed hood ornamentation are front-end presentation for 1955.

Re-engineered from the tires up, the Bel Air convertible is completely transformed in style. Power plant, suspension, steering, visibility, comfort and safety are all materially improved.

In the above view of the four-door Two Tone, note the lattice work grille, hooded headlamps, the sweep-sight windshield area and attractive chrome moulding. It is one of the 14 models for 1955.

A new push-button radio similar to the one on the Corvette is a highspot among accessories. The design is particularly appreciated on long trips when station frequencies vary with geographical locations. The radio is equipped with a bar which, when depressed, automatically tunes in stations in sequence across the dial.

Electrically driven windshield wipers are available optionally. Electric power lifts may now be specified as an option on all four windows. For 1955 control buttons are mounted beneath each window and all windows can be manipulated from the left front door. The electric front seat adjuster is again an option.

An intriguing "first" for drivers seeking high performance is a "power package" which can be purchased on V8 models. This includes a four-barrel carburetor and dual exhaust system for a consequential horsepower rating of 180.

1955 CHEVROLET SPECIFICATIONS

Engine

	Six Cylinder	Eight Cylinder
Type	In Line	V
No. of Cylinders	6	8
Bore and Stroke	3-9/16 x 3-15/16	3-3/4 x 3
Displacement	235.5	265
Brake Horsepower:		
Conventional	123 at 3800 rpm	162 at 4400
Powerglide	136 at 4200	
Compression Ratio	7.5 to 1	8.0 to 1
Taxable Horsepower	30.4	45

Transmission: Conventional and Automatic

Capacities

Oil (quarts)	5
Water (quarts)	17 with heater, 16 without heater
Gasoline (gallons)	16

General

Wheelbase	115 in.
Overall height	62.1
Overall width	74.0
Overall length	195.6
Tread (front)	58.0
Tread (rear)	58.8
Steering ratio	62.1

Six Cylinder	Eight Cylinder
Conventional Powerglide	Conventional Powerglide

1955 CHEVROLET V-8 ENGINE SPECIFICATIONS

General

Type	90° V, 8 Cylinders
Valve Arrangement	In Head
Bore and Stroke (Inches)	3-¾ x 3
Piston Displacement (Cubic Inches)	265
Firing Order	1-8-4-3-6-5-7-2
Compression Ratio	
Standard Head	8.0:1
Optional Head	N.A.
Taxable Horsepower	45
Advertised Max. Brake Horsepower at Engine Rpm.	
Standard Head	162 at 4,400
Optional Twin Carbs.	—
With Fuel (Octane and Method)	
Standard Head	—
Optional Head	—
Max. Torque (Lb. Ft. at Rpm.)	
Standard Head	257 at 2,200
Optional Twin Carbs.	—

Pistons

Description and Finish	Cam Ground, Tin Coated, Controlled Expansion, Flat Head, Slipper Type Skirt
Weight (Pistons Only—Ozs.)	18.77

Rings

Type	
No. 1	Multipiece Oil Ring
No. 2	Inside Bevel or Counterbore
No. 3	Inside Bevel or Counterbore
No. 4 Oil or Compression	None
No. of Rings Above Piston Pin	3

Piston Pins

Length	3.110-3.130
Diameter	.9270-.9273
Type	
Locked in Rod, in Piston, Floating	Pressed in Rod Bushing
In Rod or Piston	None

Connecting Rods

Weight (Ozs.)	19.02
Length (Center to Center)	5.700
Bearing	
Type	Removable
Effective Length	.817
Clearance	.0007-.0028
End Play	.008-.014 (2 Rods)

Crankshaft

Weight (Lbs.)	47.75
Vibration Damper Type	Oscillating (Rubber Floating)
End Thrust Taken by Bearing (No.)	No. 5
Crankshaft End Play	.002-.006
Main Bearing	
Type	Removable
Clearance	.0008-.0034

Camshaft

Bearings (Number)	5
Type of Drive	Chain and Sprocket

Valve System

Hydraulic Lifters (Yes or No)	Yes
Special Provision for Valve Rotation (Intake, Exhaust)	None
Rocker Ratio	1.455:1
Tappet Clearance for Timing	
Intake	—
Exhaust	Zero
Timing Marks on Flywheel, Damper, Other	Damper
Timing	
Intake	
Opens (°BTC)	18°
Closes (°ABC)	54°
Exhaust	
Opens (°BBC)	52°
Closes (°ATC)	20°
Intake	
Overall Length	4.902-4.922
Actual Overall Head Dia.	1.720
Angle of Seat	46° in Head
Stem Diameter	.3415-.3422
Lift	.324
Outer Spring Pressure and Length	
Valve Closed (Lb. at In.)	71-79 at 1.696
Valve Open (Lb. at In.)	145-155 at 1.366
Inner Spring Pressure and Length	
Valve Closed (Lb. at In.)	—
Valve Open (Lb. at In.)	—
Exhaust	
Overall Length	4.913-4.933
Actual Overall Head Dia.	1.495-1.505
Angle of Seat	46° in Head
Stem Diameter	.3410-.3417
Lift	.324
Outer Spring Press and Length	
Valve Closed (Lb. at In.)	71-79 at 1.696
Valve Open (Lb. at In.)	145-155 at 1.366
Inner Spring Press and Length	
Valve Closed (Lb. at In.)	—
Valve Open (Lb. at In.)	—

Lubrication System

Type of Lubrication (Splash, Pressure, Nozzle)	
Main Bearings	Pressure
Connecting Rods	Pressure
Piston Pins	Sprayed from Connecting Rod Journal Boss
Camshaft Bearings	Pressure
Tappets	Metered Pressure
Timing Gear or Chain	Pressure
Cylinder Walls	Pressure Jet
Oil Pump Type	Gear
Normal Oil Pressure (Lb. at Rpm.)	35 PSi. at 1,170-1,240 Rpm.
Type Oil Intake (Floating, Stationary)	Floating
Oil Filter Type (Full Flow, Partial Flow)	Partial Flow
Capacity of Crankcase, Less Filter-Refill (Qt.)	4
Oil Grade Recommended (SAE Viscosity and Temperature Range)	Not Lower than 32° F....SAE 20W or SAE 20 As Los as 10° F....SAE 20W As Low as Minus 10° F....SAE 10W Below Minus 10° F....SAE 5W
Oil Type Recommended	Heavy Duty

Fuel System

Fuel Filter (Type)	Screen
Fuel Pump	
Type (Elec. or Mech.)	Mechanical
Pressure Range	4 to 5¼ Psi.
Vacuum Booster (Std., Optl., None)	None
Carburetor	
Number Used	1
Type	
Downdraft, Side Inlet, Other	Downdraft
Single or Dual	Double Barrel
Intake Manifold Heat Control (Manual, Auto., None)	Automatic
Automatic Choke Type (Integral, Other)	Integral

Exhaust System

Type (Single, Single with Cross-over, Dual, Other)	Single with Cross-Under Pipe

Cooling System

Type (Pressure, System, Atmospheric, Other)	Pressure
Circulation Thermostat	
Starts to Open at	160°
Water Pump	
Type (Centrifugal, Other)	Centrifugal
Number of Pumps	1
Bearing Type	Double Row Ball Bearing
Water Jackets Full Length of Cylinder (Yes, No.)	Yes
Water All Around Cylinder (Yes, No)	Yes

Electrical—Supply System

Battery	
Voltage and Plates/Cell	12-9
Terminal Grounded	Negative
Generator (Type)	2 Brush, Shunt Wound
Regulator (Type)	Current and Voltage Control
Min. Gen. Rpm. Required	2,750

Electrical—Starting System

Starting Motor	
Engine Cranking Speed	N.A.
Motor Control	
Switch (Solenoid, Manual)	Solenoid
Motor Drive (Engagement Type)	Positive Shift Solenoid

Electrical—Ignition System

Distributor	
Spark Advance Data (at Distributor Shaft)	
Centr. Advance Start (Rpm.) C/S	300
Centr. Advance Max. Deg. at Rpm.	16 at 1,800 Rpm.
Vacuum Advance Start (In. Hg.)	6.0
Vacuum Advance (Max. Deg. at In. Hg.)	13¾ at 15 in Hg.
Breaker Gap (In.)	.016-.021
Timing	
C/S Deg. at Rpm.	4° BTC at Idle
Mark Location	Damper
Spark Plug	
Make and Model	AC 44-5
Gap	.033-.038

New Body, Suspension, Interior, and Powerhouse V-8 Headline Chevrolet's All-Out Bid for Top Car Position in 1955

1955 Chevrolet ROAD TEST

MOTOR *Life* Test Staff Report

CHEVROLET'S stylists, engineers and sales personnel are out to give the public exactly what they want in 1955. If the public wants an expensive-looking car, the 1955 Chevrolet resembles, more than superficially, expensive older brothers Oldsmobile, Buick, Cadillac. If it's horsepower and a new engine that's desired, Chevrolet has their new short stroke V-8 which is rated at 162 hp and with an optional power package turns out 180 hp. If it's low speed acceleration, the 1955 model Powerglide now has a low with a "snap." If it's the sleek, "low" look, the 1955 models have been reduced in height; up to six inches for the station wagons. If it's the sports car look, enthusiasts will be happy with a grille which could have originated in the Italian Ferrari factory. And if it's "feel" and cornering the buyer is looking for, Chevy's new "spherical-joint" front suspension and wider-apart rear springs will offer that. If it's economy, the proven, in-line six cylinder engine is still available—but with upped horsepower which makes no slouch of the six cylinder version—in performance.

Chevrolet lovers, who watched slightly abashed as their car took a second seat in national sales, once again have something to crow about and it's as big a story as Chevrolet's introduction of the six cylinder engine in 1929 and the subsequent change in concept of low-priced values.

The most dramatic aspect of the 1955 Chevrolet is the new look; lowered tops, hoods, belt lines and "goodies" taken directly from some of General Motors' Motorama "dream cars." The grille, a cross-mesh affair, is wide and set into a front which slopes inward from top to bottom. Headlights are completely shrouded ala Cadillac.

From the headlights back, the car is definitely GM and, judging by sales of the Oldsmobile, Cadillac and Buick, that ain't bad. The Chevy has the GM wrap-around windshield this year and it serves to only further enhance the GM relationship. Through some alchemy known only to automotive stylists, however, the car still manages to look like a Chevrolet. How the stylists have managed to change the body so drastically and still retain this look remains a great mystery to the MOTOR *Life* test staff.

Although Chevrolet will advertise two engines, there are actually four. The new V-8 (called valve-in-head by Chevrolet, known as overhead valve to the remainder of the industry) packs a compression ratio of 8:1, has a displacement of 265 cubic inches, a bore of 3.75 inches and a stroke of 3 inches; undoubtedly the shortest stroked engine in the industry today. (For complete details on the V-8 engine, see Chevrolet's New V-8 Engine story in this issue.) The standard V-8 engine, as stock in the 1955 Chevrolet, will boast 162 horsepower with a single carburetor. For speed enthusiasts, an optional "power package" is available which consists of a four-throat carburetor and dual exhausts. According to Chevrolet engineers, this raises the horsepower to 180. MOTOR *Life* test staffers didn't have the opportunity to drive the Chevrolet so equipped but will report on that model in a later issue.

The other "two" engines are the two models of Chevrolet's famous six cylinder model. The manual transmission model is available with 123 horsepower. Powerglide models come with 136 horsepower. Both are designed for maximum economy—but their performance will be not very far behind the field's V-8s.

Not content with the new horsepower and torque ratings, Chevy engineers have also supplied the American motorist with a choice of transmissions; Powerglide,

Frontal treatment of the 1955 Chevrolet features inward slope, Ferrari-type grille, hooded headlights and wrap-around bumper.

Trunk and rear fenders resemble style on Olds, Buick. Tail and backup lights are massive, slope inward under chrome hooding.

1955 Chevrolet 210 Sedan
Performance and Specifications

SPEEDOMETER ERROR

Indicated 30 mph	28.3	mph actual
Indicated 40 mph	37.7	mph actual
Indicated 50 mph	47	mph actual
Indicated 60 mph	56.4	mph actual
Indicated 70 mph	65.8	mph actual
Indicated 80 mph	75.3	mph actual
Indicated 90 mph	83.4	mph actual

ACCELERATION

0-30 mph	4.6 sec.
0-60 mph	13.9 sec.

TOP SPEED

Fastest Run (One-way only) ....98.1 mph

FUEL CONSUMPTION

At steady 30 mph ....24 mpg

ENGINE—V-8 overhead valve. Bore and stroke, 3.75 x 3. Compression ratio, 8:1. Displacement, 265 cubic inches. Advertised horsepower, 162 (180 with optional power package of dual exhausts and four-throat carburetor). Chevrolet six is also available with 123 hp for manual shift, 136 hp for Powerglide models.

REAR AXLE RATIOS—Conventional, 3.7:1. Overdrive, 4.11:1. Powerglide, 3.55:1

DIMENSIONS

Wheelbase	115"
Tread	58" Front, 58.8" Rear
Width	74.0"
Height	62.1"
Turning radius curb-to-curb	39'
Steering, turns lock to lock	5.34
Weight (shipping)	3220 lbs. with Powerglide

Plenum chamber arching across the body at the cowl feeds air into passenger compartment. Provision is made to keep rain out.

Bel Air convertible shows extent of Chevrolet restyling for 1955. Convertible combines best of GM "expensive-dream car" styling.

Instrument panel was lifted directly from the Corvette, but adds chrome mesh band. Powerglide quadrant is now at base of speedo.

standard and overdrive. The new Powerglide has been redesigned to shift more smoothly, to accelerate more rapidly. And the engineers have been successful. In a series of test runs, MOTOR *Life* test staff found that the Powerglide Chevrolet models were equal to. and in the majority of cases superior to, the manual shift models for out-and-out acceleration. Although the stick-shift model digs out from a stoplight faster, the momentary lull while shifting gears (regardless of snap shifts) allows the Powerglide model to move strongly ahead. Starting in the Powerglide "Low" range. and then shifting into Drive, provided a faster initial start but the difference is almost imperceptible. Powerglide, for '55, is quiet and effortless, maintaining the best of the "shift-less" transmission feel. Above 20 mph, the transmission digs in sharply and the Chevy V-8 accelerates from 20 to 60 like a well-tuned sports car. The old "American low-priced stocks won't hit 100" attitude of speed enthusiasts is closer than ever to oblivion, for the Powerglide-equipped Chevy turned in a fastest one-way run of 98 mph. With a spot of tuning and/or with the optional speed kit, the car should easily exceed the magic 100 mph mark.

The 1955 Chevrolet feels as good as it looks. Lower to the ground, with a vastly improved suspension, the car stays snug to the road at all speeds up to 70 mph. Over that figure, there is a little sidesway and the passenger car type of springing shows up when the car hits bumps at high speed. The new ball-joint front suspension holds the wheels tight into curves and bends, regardless of heel-over in the body. Drivers who navigate curves by the seat of their pants will find that less caution will have to be used when diving into corners and negotiating tricky mountain roads. The test car had power steering as standard equipment and the reduced amount of wheel travel gave test drivers the impression that they were handling a car which had been especially set up for the Mexican Road Race.

In the rear, Chevrolet engineers have added to the stability of the passenger cars by adding nine inches to the length of rear springs, giving them a total length of 58 inches. By repositioning those springs further outboard of the chassis, the engineers have indicated that the Chevrolet Corvette made a good test study car, for it is a move directly from that model.

One of the most unusual aspects of the new suspension system is Chevrolet's anti-dive factor. A control arm geometry cancels out most of the objectionable nose-spin aspects of braking. The 1955 Chevrolet rolls to a flat, level stop—in controlled braking procedures. Comparison photograph shows the difference between the "tails up" attitude of the '54 and the level '55 when quickly braked at the same speed.

One interesting model driven by the MOTOR *Life* test staff was the overdrive-equipped standard transmission sedan. Long desired by many Chevrolet owners, *overdrive* Chevrolets were rare. Owners were forced to order overdrive units from outside manufacturers, have them installed at home. Now, Chevrolet has made an overdrive unit optional equipment. This unit substitutes a high performance 4.11:1 rear axle ratio for the 3.7:1 ratio which is normal with the standard transmission. Test instruments showed that the Chevrolet engine, when in the overdrive range, was working 22 percent less and was actually turning over 600 engine revolutions less per mile at moderate cruising speeds.

Frame for the Chevrolet V-8 uses a new design, stiffer side members and a better placement of engine mounts. Side members of the strengthened frame have been located over a foot further apart at the narrowest point and have been brought four inches closer together in the rear.

In an interview with a frame engineer, the MOTOR *Life* test staff learned that the new frame had been built with engine vibration and a resistance to frame twist in mind. To reduce engine vibration, the new engine is now mounted on four, instead of last year's three, mounts. The front mounts are the strut-type and are attached to brackets on each side of the cylinder block at the lower corners. Rear mounts are located

Chevrolet Bel Air hardtop will probably be the most sought-after model. New Chevy V-8, with "power package" turns out 180 hp.

between the lower rear edges of the clutch housing and short brackets cantilevered from the frame side members. Rubber insulation is used heavily—and is effective. When idling, the Chevrolet engine is noiseless and vibrationless and at 65 mph, the only vibration to enter the passenger compartment stems directly from road conditions.

Glass area in the four door sedans totals a surprising 24.5 square feet—a lot of visibility for any car. Partial addition to this is the new wrap-around windshield which, in itself, increases windshield area 19 percent alone. Visibility across the flat hood is excellent, although the upward-sloped hood could have been designed in reverse to allow more "close" visibility to the car.

Inside the cockpit, the Chevrolet looks and feels "different." Ammeter and oil gauges have been dropped from the dashboard and replaced with red warning lights, like other competitive makes. The glove compartment has been moved to the dash center. Dash also includes a lighted quadrant for shifting the Powerglide at night. Shift mechanism on the steering post, long an eyesore in Chevrolet models, has finally been encased in one unit with the steering post. Pedals are hung in a style which was very successful for a competitor last year. The dash, itself, is a direct lift from Chevrolet's Corvette sports car but has had a wide band of chrome mesh added to it. An overhanging shelf protects the driver from chrome-glare but the painted dash shelf introduces reflections. The speedometer housing is V-shaped with a semi-circular top. At the other end of the dash, another circle-topped V shape encloses the radio loudspeaker. Acoustically, this placement could be vastly improved. The test car was equipped with the GM push-bar tuning radio which automatically searches out the strongest signal when a button is depressed. Although ideal for keeping eyes on the road, the push-bar radio tuner, unless adjusted, has the annoying habit of stopping every fraction of an inch in highly congested areas with many radio stations, stopping not at all during the night out in the country where most signals are too weak.

Fresh air is introduced into the passenger compartment through an exterior cowl-wide intake, fashioned after Big Brother's. Provisions have been made to keep the incoming air dry and although the test crew did some of their stints during one of those summer showers, the incoming air stayed dry, did turn cool. This will solve the long standing problem of interior cooling during thunderstorms when an open win-

(Continued on page 31)

1955 models have ball-joint front suspension with "anti-dive" features. Note how '55 model stays level, '54 "dives" braking.

New Chevrolet Turbo-Fire V-8 features short stroke of 3" and bore of 3.75". Displacement of the 162 hp engine is 265 cu. in.

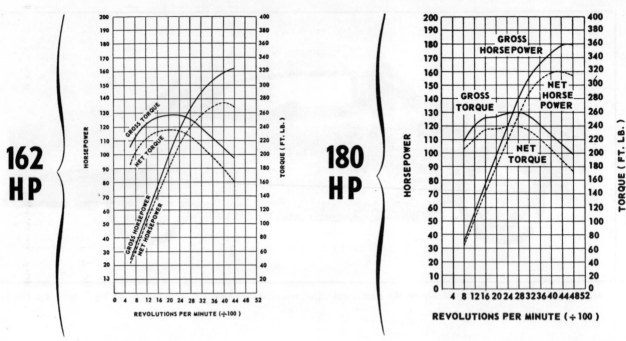

162 HP ... **180 HP**

New Chevrolet engine turns out 162 hp in stock form and 180 hp with special manifold, dual exhausts and four throat carburetors. Power/ weight ratio is 18:1. Comparison charts for the 162 hp and the 180 hp engines show development of torque and horsepower at various rpm.

CHEVROLET'S

THE V-8 must be here to stay ... Chevrolet is using one at last!

I don't think it's exaggerating anything to say that overall production in the Chevrolet organization is more efficient, well planned, and economical than anywhere else in the industry. It just about *has* to be. Their physical size and "break-even" volume are greater than the others and, unlike Ford, they've got to crank out a hefty enough profit to keep a bunch of hungry stockholders happy. It's sink or swim in a big way at Chevy.

The point I want to make is this: We can study the design of the new Chevrolet V-8 engine and safely say, "Here is the last word in producing a complicated 8 cylinder engine at a price competitive with the most inexpensive powerplants in the industry." Furthermore, I think it only fair that we approach our design analysis *expecting* that some points on performance, durability, etc. might be compromised to hold down that *first cost*. We can't expect this to be any custom-built jewel for a utility family car; it is, instead, the very best mass-production compromise between cost and functional efficiency that modern bread-and-butter engineering can devise.

Let's judge it from this angle ...

A MODERN V-8

At first glance a cross-section of the new 1955 Chevrolet V-8 looks quite a lot like the Olds Rocket and Cadillac engines. We see the familiar G.M. Research wedge-type combustion chamber with in-line overhead valves, oversquare stroke/ bore ratio, slipper pistons, and the crank-case chopped at the main bearing center lines.

With a bore and stroke of 3¾" x 3" (265 cu. in.), the stroke/bore ratio of .8:1 is equal with Buick as the lowest in the industry. This not only permits an overall engine width of only 26½", but the wide bore makes room for large valves *in relation to the cylinder displacement.* (This last advantage of the oversquare layout is not generally appreciated by John Q., but it's actually a very important factor in the terrific performance we're getting out of our new ohv V-8s these days.) The large 1¾" intake valves in conjunction with huge ports give really deep breathing, even though we're pulling through a two throat carburetor. The peak output ratings of 162 hp at 4400 rpm and 257 lb.-ft. rated torque at 2200 rpm attest to this. (These figures were achieved running stripped on the dynamometer; maximum output as installed in the car runs about 137 hp, according to factory data.) At any rate, this is a lot of punch from an inexpensive utility passenger car engine of 265 cu. in.; we can attribute it mainly to the good porting, healthy compression ratio of 8.0:1, and the very short stroke, which reduces the

power lost in friction. I'd say the mill should easily hold its own against the other low-priced V-8s on performance and fuel economy.

SQUEEZING THE NICKEL

The thing that impressed me most about the new Chevrolet design were the many brilliant features aimed solely at reducing the *cost of manufacturing* the thing. I was flabbergasted, in fact. The thing is a work of genius from this angle. I'd bet they can build it for little over *half* of what it costs Ford and Plymouth to build their new V-8s. Space won't permit a complete discussion of this interesting aspect, but here are just a few of the cost-saving features:

The cylinder heads for each bank are *interchangeable* and are made on the same machines. There are no separate valve guides; the valves run direct in the iron heads. (This idea was originated by Ford Motor Co.) The piston pin is pressed into the top end of the rod, eliminating need for a bushing here, as with a floating pin, and even eliminating the slot and screw clamp as on the Chevy 6.

There are no rocker arm shafts on the new Chevrolet engine! That's right. The rockers are light one-piece steel stampings that oscillate on crude steel-on-steel ball joints supported by studs pressed in the heads. The fulcrum ball is held on the stud by a nut and lock-screw; valve lash

16

LATEST GM ENGINE
FEATURES LOW
PRODUCTION COST AND
A DIFFERENT APPROACH
TO THE OHV V-8

BY ROGER HUNTINGTON, SAE

Cutaway side view of new V-8 shows compactness of design. Moving parts are factory balanced after assembly. Engine features ease of repair.

NEW V-8

New V-8 runs a compression of 8:1, has a displacement of 265 cubic in. Manufacturing costs for new engine have been reduced to the minimum.

adjustment with the solid lifters is merely a matter of turning the nut. Pushrods are steel tubing, crimped at the ends, operating in hollowed-out seats in the rocker stampings. The new Chevrolet intake manifold casting is unique in that it serves not only as the manifold, but also seals the tappet chamber, contains cast-in water outlet passages from the two heads, and directs these to a central point where the thermostat is located. All other V-8s use a separate tappet chamber cover plate.

The entire lubrication system is a matter of drilled holes and machined passages in the block and head castings; there are no external pipes. The main oil gallery runs above the camshaft. Oil is fed down to the five cam bearings through drilled holes; most of it, however, is routed *around* the cam bearing through an "annulus" passage to the main bearing below—from where it's also fed off to the rods. Slots at the split lines of the rods throw oil off on the cylinder walls once each revolution. Each row of valve lifters (hydraulic lifters are used with the Powerglide transmission) has its own special oil gallery, running at reduced pressure by routing the oil through a metering slot; oil is fed into the lifter, then up through the hollow pushrod where it squirts out to lubricate the valve mechanism in the head. The oil drains back

(Continued on page 31)

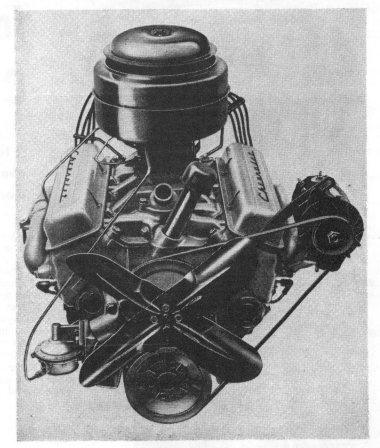

Below: Chevrolet follows the swing to multi-barrel carburettors with a twin-barrel type for its V-8. It has an automatic choke.

Above: Rectangular frame is said to have more resistance to twisting than old model, although it is one-fifth lighter. This is a six-cylinder version of the car.

From the Editors of "Popular Science", who reviewed the first models.

Below: Red warning lights have replaced the ammeter and oil gauge on the instrument panel.

162 h.p. V-8 ENGINE for AMERICAN CHEVROLET

A long-awaited motor change for one of the world's best-known cars.

WITH a new V-8 engine, the 1955 Chevrolet has made a dashing entrance on to the automotive stage.

The new valve-in-head V-8 puts out 162 horsepower, 37 horses more than Chevrolet's biggest six of 1954 could muster. The car it drives comes equipped for the first time with tubeless tyres and a 12-volt electrical system.

Air conditioning is available as optional equipment for the V-8 line.

The car will not be available in Australia.

A lower silhouette, 2½ inches closer to the ground, makes the new Chevrolet look longer although the wheelbase is unchanged for 1955 at 115 inches.

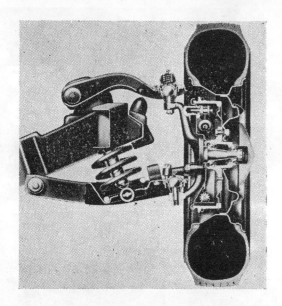

Above: Front suspension, also altered, has ball joints instead of swivel pins, and inclined coil springs with a tubular shock absorbers to control them inside.

Above: Chevrolet has experimented with V-8's since 1917. Present engine combines short stroke and large bore.

There are certain G.M. family traits in the features of the '55 Chevvy—the tapered doors that made their debut on the first Buick Skylark, the vertical windshield pillars, wrap-around windshields and high, straight mudguard crowns that became familiar sights on recent Buicks and Oldsmobiles. Its hooded headlights are an inheritance from G.M. dream cars of the past two years.

The compact new Chevrolet V-8 engine (called the "Turbo-Fire") has a compression ratio of 8 to 1, as opposed to the 7.5-to-1 ratio of that of last year's engines. It has a bore of 3.75 inches and a stroke of 3 inches, shortest in the U.S.

Capacity is 4.3 litres. It weighs 30 pounds *less* than the less-powerful sixes.

There is no rocker gear. Each push rod and its accompanying valve stem are attached to a pivot which rocks on a stud rising from the block.

On test, the engine will run to 5,200 r.p.m. without valve bounce or breakages.

For the restless owner who is not wholly satisfied with his V-8's innate 162 horsepower, there is available a package kit, consisting of a four-barrel carburettor and dual-exhaust system, that will boost the horse-power to 180!

In addition to the V-8 Chevrolet continues to offer two sixes. Both have had their power boosted for 1955.

The six-cylinder engine that comes with conventional gearshift now has 123 horsepower, an increase of eight over the 1954 figure.

The six built to go with Chevrolet's Powerglide automatic transmission has been upped to 136 horse-power, 11 better than last year's output.

For the first time Chevrolet will install an over-drive which automatically cuts in above 31 miles an hour when the driver takes his foot off the accelerator.

As a natural result of providing what Chevrolet calls a "sweep-sight" windshield, front-seat visibility in the 1955 cars has been increased by 19 per cent. In the four-door sedans, with every window larger than ever, there is now 24.5 square feet of glass area.

'55 Chevrolet V8

A new engine, exceptional handling, and many other features

In a full-power turn, it's easy to keep control. Here the Chevy shows its good maneuverability as front tire rolls under

Driving a Chevy was never like this. Wrap-around windshield is only the beginning; hood is now low, fenders high

By Walt Woron

WE'VE JUST FINISHED road testing the new '55 Chevy, and our heads are buzzing. After doing one of these road tests, it's sometimes hard to know what to write about first. Should we talk about the car's acceleration, its brakes, its handling? Or discuss its interior, its styling, its ride?

With the '55 Chevy the decision is harder than usual to make, because there are so many good features about the car. It has exceptional handling qualities for an American production car. Its acceleration is better than all but the top performance

cars of '54. Its ride is improved over last year's model. So where do you start? Well, how about at the beginning? We'll go to the Chevrolet Zone Office in Detroit, Mich., pick up the Two-Ten four-door sedan waiting for us, and go from there.

Before we get in, let's walk around the car and inspect the **general workmanship.** The panels all seem to fit fairly well, there aren't any ripples in the body, there's only the barest amount of orange peel in the paint. The grille will take some extra work if you want to keep it shining; looks like you'll need a bottle brush to keep each square clean. The wrap-around bumpers should protect the corners of the fenders, while the bumper guards look sturdy enough to cope with today's traffic-banging. The 6.70 x 15 tires are the new U.S. Royal or Goodrich tubeless (standard on *all* models).

We've commended Chevrolet for years on their clever tool tie-down arrangement in the **trunk compartment.** Let's see if they still have it this year. Putting the key into the lock and giving it a twist is all that's necessary for the deck to lift gently; it takes only one hand to do the trick. There's the bumper jack and lug wrench next to the spare tire, but closer and fitted into a groove that will keep

it from bouncing around. The arrangement is even better in this new version, since it makes more stowage space this way.

There's plenty of room inside the trunk (20 cubic feet of it), while the rubber mat is practical from the standpoint of durability. Metal panels on the sides are also more durable than the more-frequent cardboard panels.

Last year we said that we expected the V8 engine to "join the crammed-engine-room set." So let's take a look at this amazing **engine** and see if we were right. The hood release is in the center, below the chrome bar; notice that with one hand it releases, and lifts of its own accord? That's balance. Notice also that the hinge is a ratchet affair that lets you lock it into position so you never need fear that the hood will suddenly come down and whack you on the head? There's no sound-deadening material under the hood, but maybe they don't need it. We'll see.

That engine is a surprise; things are much more accessible than we thought possible. The generator is right out on top, in front. The fuel pump is low, but you can get to it and work around it. The oil dipstick isn't hard to reach, and oil filling (for you home mechanics) is a cinch. Take off the carburetor air cleaner,

MT's customary testing equipment (not attached in this photo) leaves abundance of room in the large trunk compartment

Headroom and legroom are not overlooked in testing the car. There's ample leg space with front seat fully rearward

Another new feature this year is the central glove compartment, easy to reach for the driver and both his passengers

Photos by
Bob MacKenzie

Engine compartment is compact, though placement of spark plugs (below hand) is awkward, especially with engine hot

If you like to putter around your new car, or if you really take it apart, Chevy ranks high as promising weekend hobby

and you can work easily on both the carburetor and distributor. The battery is right out where it will remind the service station attendant to fill it. Valve adjustments should be easy. Plug changing is the one nasty chore; they're located under the exhaust manifolds, so don't try to get at them while the engine is still hot.

That completes our outside inspection, so let's get **inside the car.** Notice how wide the door swings open? Stays open, too. You'll be able to park this car on any incline, open the door, get out with an armload of packages, and not fear that the door will close suddenly on you.

The seat seems fairly soft, yet firm enough not to be tiring on long trips. There's plenty of headroom (even with a hat on), good shoulder room and hiproom (more this year than last, in fact), and fair legroom. The seat adjusts easily enough on its track, but there's not enough movement rearward (there's only 4.4 inches) for six-footers. With the front seat all the way back, let's get in the rear seat and see how that is for comfort.

The rear doors open almost at 90 degrees to the car and stay open the same way. When you close them you can push down the button, locking the door handle so you can't open it unless you pull up the button again—not new, but still a good safety item, especially if you have young children. Notice also that the front seat-back springs are covered? That'll keep you from barking your knees and your children from hurting their hands or faces on sudden stops that may throw them against the seat.

TEST CAR AT A GLANCE
'55 Chevrolet V8 Two-Ten with Powerglide

REAR WHEEL HORSEPOWER
(Determined on Clayton chassis dynamometer. All tests are made under full load, which is similar to climbing a hill at full throttle. Observed hp figures not corrected to standard atmospheric conditions.)

49	road hp @ 1800 rpm and 24	mph
57	road hp @ 2000 rpm and 32	mph
67	road hp @ 2500 rpm and 52	mph
Max. 78	road hp @ 3200 rpm and 69	mph

TOP SPEED
(In miles per hour over surveyed ¼-mile.)
Fastest one-way run	97.8
Slowest one-way run	96.3
Average of four runs	97.3

ACCELERATION
(In seconds; checked with fifth wheel and electric speedometer.)
Standing start ¼-mile (71 mph)	19.0
0-30 mph	4.3
0-60 mph	12.3
10-30 mph	3.1
30-50 mph	4.4
50-80 mph	15.5

SPEEDOMETER ERROR
(Checked with fifth wheel and electric speedometer.)
Car speedometer read 29	@ true 30 mph
44	@ true 45 mph
60	@ true 60 mph
76	@ true 75 mph
101	@ top speed

FUEL CONSUMPTION
(In miles per gallon; checked with fuel flowmeter, fifth wheel, and electric speedometer. Mobilgas Special used.)
Steady 30 mph	20.6
Steady 45 mph	19.2
Steady 60 mph	15.8
Stop-and-go driving over measured course	13.7
Tank average for 1241 miles	14.5

STOPPING DISTANCE
(To the nearest foot; checked with electrically actuated detonator.)
30 mph	33
45 mph	82
60 mph	146

'55 Chevrolet Road Test

John Booth and MT's Editor attach Ethyl Corp.'s fifth wheel to test car to obtain exact facts and figures on gas mileage

Headroom is good back here too (again with a hat), while shoulder room is also good. You'd have to be pretty tall and wear size 17 shoes before you'd run out of room to stretch your legs and push your feet under the front seat.

Let's get started before we inspect any more of the car. The rest we'll catch on the road during our testing.

Since this test Chevy has Powerglide we'll have to move the selector lever to P (parking) or N (neutral) before it'll start. (See the quadrant down at the bottom of the instrument cluster? It's been moved from the steering column.) Now we switch on the key-starter (which you can do without a key if you're forgetful and leave the switch in OFF instead of LOCK position). The engine starts right away, and purrs healthily. It seems quieter than many V8s. We can disengage the cane-type emergency brake with our left hand by twisting it slightly and pushing it forward, keeping our left foot on the pendulum foot brake, and moving the selector to D (drive). The engine is idling a trifle slow, so the generator warning light is burning red. As we give it a bit of throttle, the light goes off and we move ahead.

The wrap-around windshield is a big improvement in **vision**: we can see both front fenders with ease. At the far side of the windshield, there's a slight amount of distortion. Moving outside, we find that it's raining, and turn on the wipers. They operate smoothly and sweep into the previously unswept areas (on '54 GM cars) next to the reverse posts. The rear view mirror doesn't block vision; on the other hand, it should be wider, to take full advantage of the wide rear window. Looking to the rear, there's no blind spot to the right of the window. We can see *both* rear fenders without rising up in the seat. That's a big help in parking, particularly in tight spots. Vision of this order was not common to previous Chevys.

You notice that the steering wheel seems to have been lowered and made more vertical? Doesn't interfere with your legs, either. The top portion of the full-circle horn ring blocks out part of the semi-circular speedometer, but wouldn't you rather crane around it once in a while instead of feeling in vain for a half-circle horn ring when you have the wheel in any position but dead ahead? Aside from this one factor, the white-on-black speedometer is easy to read, and as it's high on the painted panel (which would be better if it were duller), you don't have to drop your eyes far from the road ahead to see it. The same holds true for the other two instruments: fuel gauge and water temperature. (Later, we found the instruments were easy to read at night and no lights glared on the windshield.)

And now to Funston Chevrolet, where we'll leave the car in the capable hands of George Bente (assistant service manager) who will install our fuel flowmeter, tachometer, vacuum gauge, and brake-testing equipment. After that we'll join Detroit Editor Don MacDonald and John Booth (builder of the X-Ray Special—see Oct. '54 MT) and be on the way to our various testing spots. During all of our testing we'll keep a close check on tank mileage, note how the car performs and handles over all roads, city streets, paved highways, dirt backroads—and from the looks of the weather, in rain, sunshine and snow.

Under normal procedure, the first thing we'd do (when working out of our home office) with a car ready for testing would be to take it to the Clayton Manufacturing Company in El Monte, Calif., for a chassis dynamometer check. Being in Detroit posed a problem, because dynamometers—and their resulting readings—vary from place to place. Thus, we took this test car to the logical place—the Clayton plant in Detroit—to obtain a reading that would compare with results of later, California-based tests.

Now, since this 162-hp, Powerglide-equipped Chevy has 1692 miles on it, let's roll out to our **top speed** strip and see what it will do. On our way there, we'll watch for other things, like body drafts (which it doesn't have), wind noise (which is fairly high above 60 mph with the quarter windows open), unusual noises (it has a driveshaft hum between 40-65 mph when you hit the throttle), ride, and handling.

You'll remember that last year we complained that the '54 Chevy floundered a bit over an unexpected dip at 40 mph. This year's car has been improved considerably in this regard. It recovers rapidly over dips with very little oscillation, and it isn't until it hits speeds of 70-80 mph that it sort of wallows after coming out of a dip. At around this same speed is where its feeling of solidness falls off, "wind wander" begins and it feels a bit light. Tar strips or rough road surfaces are audible, but the driver doesn't feel it through the steering wheel. (Undercoating would certainly help here.) You'll notice that sidesway won't bother you.

This '55 Chevy doesn't let any moss grow under its feet: an average of 97.3 mph is not only adequate in itself, a good five mph faster than last year's car (also equipped with Powerglide), but is faster than any '54 car in its class. The overdrive car (with a higher final rear axle ratio of 2.88 to 1 vs. 3.55 to 1 for Powerglide) should be slightly faster, and when that's coupled with the 180-hp engine, the Chevy should easily break 100.

Acceleration-wise, this car's got it, too! Can you imagine a Chevy outdigging every '54 car but a Cadillac and Buick Century, and being able to stay with a Chrysler, Lincoln and Oldsmobile? We couldn't believe it either after just one

'55 CHEVROLET V8 TWO-TEN WITH POWERGLIDE

GENERAL SPECIFICATIONS

ENGINE: Ohv V8. Bore 3¾ in. Stroke 3 in. Stroke/bore ratio 0.8:1. Compression ratio 8.0:1. Displacement 265 cu. in. Advertised bhp 162 @ 4400 rpm (180 bhp @ 4600 rpm optional). Bhp per cu. in. .611. Piston travel @ max. bhp 2200 ft. per min. Max. bmep 146.2 psi. Max. torque 257 ft. lb. @ 2200 rpm (260 ft. lb. @ 2800 rpm optional). **DRIVE SYSTEM:** STANDARD transmission is three-speed synchromesh using helical gears. RATIOS: 1st 2.94, 2nd 1.68, 3rd 1.00, reverse 2.94. AUTOMATIC transmission is Powerglide, three-element torque converter with planetary gears. Maximum converter ratio at stall 2.1. RATIOS: Drive 1.82 x converter ratio and torque converter only, Low and Reverse 1.82 x converter ratio. OVERDRIVE transmission is standard shift with planetary gearset. RATIO: 0.7. **REAR AXLE RATIOS:** Standard 3.70, Automatic 3.55, Overdrive 4.11. **DIMENSIONS:** Wheelbase 115 in. Tread 58 front, 58½ rear. Wheelbase/tread ratio 1.96:1. Overall width 74 in. Overall length 195⅝ in. Overall height (empty) 62¹⁄₁₀ in. Turning diameter 38 ft. Turns lock to lock 4½. Test car weight 3470 lbs. Test car

weight/bhp ratio 21.4:1. Weight distribution 52.7% front, 47.3% rear. Tire size 6.70 x 15, tubeless. **PRICES:** (Including suggested retail price at main factory, federal tax, and delivery and handling charges, but not freight.) ONE-FIFTY, utility sedan $1692, two-door sedan $1784, four-door sedan $1827, two-door station wagon $2129. TWO-TEN, club coupe $1934, two-door sedan $1874, four-door sedan $1918, two-door station wagon $2178, four-door station wagon $2226. BEL AIR, two-door sedan $1987, four-door sedan $2031, hardtop $2166, convertible $2305, four-door station wagon $2361. (Six-cylinder models $99 less.) **ACCESSORIES:** Powerglide $178, overdrive $108, "Plus-Power" kit (dual exhaust system, four-throat carburetor, special air cleaner and intake manifold) $59, power steering $92, power brakes $38, power seat with automatic window lifts $145, radios $62, $84, and $111, air conditioning $565, heaters $48 and $73, white sidewall tires (exchange) $27. **PARTS AND LABOR COSTS and ESTIMATED COST PER MILE** for the Chevrolet V8 Two-Ten will appear in an early issue.

For assurance that hood will stay in place while you do engine work, ratchet-type hinge provides a positive hood stop

run, so repeated it again and again. The combination of electric speedometer, fifth wheel, and the bank of stopwatches just doesn't lie. There is no point in using LOW, then manually shifting to DRIVE; automatic shift comes at peak rpm (4400) and 55 mph. Incidentally, we could practically read the car's speedometer instead of the electric one for all the error in it; it isn't more than one mph off until it gets well above 75 mph.

The automatic upshift, even under full throttle, is smooth, while downshifts are practically unnoticeable. To downshift manually, you can move the lever to LOW, but it won't go into that gear until the speed has dropped to approximately 55 mph (as a protection against over-revving). At any speed under 55 mph, shoving the throttle all the way to the floorboard will downshift the transmission to LOW, giving you a terrific boot. The Powerglide in this car is much quieter than that of the '54 Chevy.

Let's try **highway passing acceleration**. It really has it here, hasn't it? The average of 4.4 seconds from 30 to 50 mph is *less than all* '54 test cars, and only five cars were faster in their 50 to 80 acceleration. Its acceleration factor seems to drop off above 70, requiring almost the same time to reach 80 mph from 70 (7.4 seconds), as it takes to go from 50 to 70 (8.1 seconds). The 15.5-second time from 50 to 80 is 12.8 seconds less than for the '54 Chevy.

Now, with level roads and no wind, we can get our steady-speed **fuel consumption** figures. (Since we encountered pinging when we used regular gas, we switched to Mobilgas Special, despite Chevrolet's claim that this car should run on regular gas. It could be set up to run on regular,

but performance would undoubtedly suffer.) After running a good number of checks at various speeds, it's obvious that the '55 Chevy has a flatter fuel economy curve than that of the '54 Six. It gives less mileage at the lower speeds, about the same at the mid-speed ranges (45 and 60), and slightly more at 75 mph. Traffic fuel economy and overall tank mileage are slightly down, in comparison to the '54 car.

The **brakes** perform as they should in a car like this. Stopping distances are less than those required for the '54. In making panic stops from 60 mph, with all wheels locked, it keeps a straight course, beginning to swerve only at the very end (when it's easy to control). The suspended pedal makes for easy left-foot braking, but it's not low enough to let you pivot your right foot on the heel from the throttle. The fact that there's much less brake dive is better for two reasons: it helps to keep passengers on their seats during sudden stops; and the reduced pivoting-action is less annoying to passengers.

If you read our driving impressions of the Chevy (Dec. '54 MT) you'll recall that we raved about **the way the car handles**. After being with us in this Chevy for 10 days, you'll have to agree that this car can be stacked up against many so-called sports cars, won't you?

Remember that we didn't have to correct the wheel on a straight road unless there was a crown? How easy it was to steer, even with our fingers (and this wasn't a power steering car)? That when we deliberately drove it off the shoulder the car would move aside, but wouldn't whip so as to cause us to lose control? That the same thing happened on streetcar tracks and ruts?

When we took it intentionally too fast

through corners, all four wheels would drift, indicating understeer. We made the rear end break loose, but only by hitting the brakes hard, locking the wheels, forcing it to start spinning. Even before we applied more power, we could correct its slide by turning into it. Taking our foot off the brake and then punching the throttle brought it completely out of the spin. This, and whipping the steering when we were going down a road at 55 mph, allowing the car then to seek its own straight course, indicates good inherent front end stability.

You'll recall that we commented that there wasn't any wheel vibration until we started over rough roads. We could throw it into corners at practically any speed and take it through without any concern— even through turns that would make most other cars quail. And best of all, we didn't have to *fight* it through the turns.

After going along with us on this 1241-mile road test, we know you'll agree that the Chevrolet (with particular credit going to Chief Engineer Ed Cole and his able staff) is quite a combination: a good-looking car (in the modern sense), plenty of top-notch performance that will constantly keep the bigger cars in track shoes, agility in traffic, sports car-acteristics as far as handling is concerned, ease of driving, a ride that isn't sacrificed on the altar of roadability, better-than-average brakes and fair fuel economy. It's a lot, especially when you add the fact that many people continue to buy Chevrolets by name alone. The greatest compliment we could pay to this car is that our praise is so high and our criticisms so minor that we find it hard to believe it's a descendant of previous Chevrolets.　　—*Walt Woron.*

Testing the Chevrolet V-8

with power-package and high performance axle

A FTER 25 years of building conservative six-cylinder automobiles, the 1955 Chevrolet V-8 is an anomaly. Accurate performance figures on 1955 cars are not yet available, but it certainly appears that a Chevrolet V-8 with optional 180 bhp engine and 4.11 axle will out-accelerate any American car on the market today!

Just how "hot" is this car? At the time our performance tests began the odometer read only 1451 miles. Yet an average of 3

The "power-package" includes a four-barrel carburetor and dual exhausts at $60 extra

tests from zero to 60 mph (actual, not indicated) gave 9.7 seconds. Perhaps a new Buick Century or Olds 88, with stick-shift, can equal this time, but our acceleration checks were severely handicapped by the redesigned shift control mechanism—the one serious fault in this car. It was absolutely impossible to make a fast shift from first to second and given a decent shift lever linkage, we are confident that the zero to 60 time can be reduced to 9.2 seconds without speed shifting.

Aside from the fantastic acceleration of the new Chevrolet V-8, perhaps the most interesting discovery was that the car would go faster in its conventional high gear than in overdrive. (See data panel.) A little slide rule work (later) showed that 104.7 mph in the 4.11 ratio requires 5360 rpm, while 102.1 in the 2.88 overdrive gear is equivalent to only 3680 rpm. The 180 bhp engine actually develops 160 net bhp at 4400 rpm when installed and operating with all accessories. In either case the engine was operating at a little over 700 rpm "off the peak" of 4400 rpm, and in overdrive, there just aren't enough horses at 3680 rpm to pull the car up to a higher top speed.

A remarkable demonstration can be made using the second-overdrive ratio of 4.78. One hundred mph can be shown on the speedometer, equivalent to an actual 94 mph and 5600 rpm. This engine speed is valve bounce rpm with the mechanical type valve lifters. The engine is absolutely smooth and silent at all speeds up to the maximum and Mr. Ed Cole, Chevrolet's Chief Engineer, tells us that one test engine ran at 5500 for 35 hours.

Sheer performance is one thing, but has not been obtained by sacrificing other desirable qualities of a family type car. The engine has tremendous torque at low speed. Second gear starts are easy on the clutch and nearly as rapid as when using low. Pickup from 10 mph in high gear is like being in second gear of previous cars. The highway cruising speed can be as high as you like and the engine is so smooth and quiet at 90 mph, indicated, that it is difficult to tell whether direct drive or overdrive is being used at the time. Nor is economy sacrificed. The over-all average for over 300 miles of varied driving was 20.4 mpg. This run included cruising at 80 mph, occasionally hitting 90, getting 100 mph indicated in second-overdrive and using the kickdown for acceleration bursts.

Like all American cars the road-holding is steady on straight roads, requires skill and dexterity on winding roads. Our experience with late model Chevrolets is not sufficient to state whether the '55 handles better than in previous years, as is claimed. Perhaps it does, but there is plenty of room for improvement in this department. Roll angle in a fast turn is about normal for an American car. The steering can be criticized, for it requires about 4.5 turns lock to lock. We say "about," because there was so much flexibility in the steering mechanism that a careless check, without watching the front wheels, would give 5.0 turns lock to lock.

The curb weight of 3390 lbs. given in the data panel includes radio and heater, items which are not included in the factory list price. The price and weight do include the **power-pack and overdrive. The wire wheels** and premium tires were borrowed from the dealer's personal Corvette, added a few extra pounds, and of course are not included in the list price.

Some idea of the extent of changes made in the 1955 Chevrolet can be conveyed by noting that of 5000 principal parts (not including standard parts like bolts, screws, etc.) 3,800 are completely new. Items which are strange or revolutionary for Chevrolet include:

1. High power to weight ratio
2. The new V-8 engine option
3. Peak torque at 2800 rpm (V-8)
4. No valve guides (V-8)
5. Floating oil intake
6. Tubular push rods (V-8)
7. Timing chain instead of gears (V-8)
8. 12 volt electrical system
9. B.W. overdrive optional
10. Open propellor shaft
11. Rear axle "steering"
12. Ball type front suspension
13. Brake dive reduced 50%
14. No anti-roll bar

Using advertised horsepower and actual curb weight, 18.9 lbs/bhp is bettered only by two or three American cars. The fact that this car will probably out-perform all of them is attributable to the high performance axle ratio of 4.11. Such a ratio is, in turn, feasible and practical only because of the short stroke, high rpm engine. The new V-8 is a far cry from the days of the prewar "cast iron six" which peaked at 3200 rpm, would not exceed a timed 80 mph — and never seemed to wear out. Yet the new V-8 should not bear the stigma commonly associated with a "high speed" engine. It peaks at a high speed, but engine revolutions per car mile are no different from the old "slow speed" Chevrolets from 1932 to 1952. More to the point, that all-important wear and durability factor, piston speed, has been drastically reduced. The really strange aspect of the Chevrolet picture is that for years they needed an overdrive and were ideally situated to use one to good advantage (high torque, low rpm 6). Now we have a V-8 that doesn't need an overdrive, and it's available. Of course the six is still produced and reference to page 13 will give performance data on the 1954 six. There is no reason to believe that the 1955 six will perform any better than the '54 model, but the overdrive with 4.11 axle will add 11% to the performance factor.

What do we especially recommend, when buying a Chevrolet? With the six, the overdrive is a good investment, whereas the V-8 with standard 3.70 axle and no overdrive would be our choice. Either car could easily be converted to a floor shift as per our article in Jan. '54, page 39. A longer pitman arm is definitely indicated as 3.5 turns lock to lock would make the car much safer in an emergency and easier to drive for hour after hour at high speed. The optional power steering on this car is completely unnecessary.

Finally, a word of appreciation to the local dealer who made this test possible. At a time when a V-8 with power-pack and overdrive was absolutely unobtainable, the Harry Mann Chevrolet Company managed to do it —by ordering the pack from the factory and installing it on an overdrive 210 club coupe. They even supplied us with a driver, Mr. Frank Milne, their General Manager. ●

ROAD AND TRACK ROAD TEST NO. A-2-55
CHEVROLET V-8 COUPE (with Power Pack and Overdrive)

SPECIFICATIONS

List price	$2285
Wheelbase	115 in.
Tread, front	58.0 in.
rear	58.8 in.
Tire size	6.70 - 15
Curb weight	3390 lbs.
distribution	53/47
Test weight	3710 lbs.
Engine	V-8
Valves	pohv
Bore & stroke	3.75 x 3.0 in.
Displacement	265 cu in. (4344 cc)
Compression ratio	8.00
Horsepower	180
peaking speed	4600
equiv. mph in od	128
Torque, ft/lbs.	260
peaking speed	2800
equiv. mph in od	77.7
Mph per 1000 rpm (od)	27.8
Mph at 2500 fpm (od)	139
Gear ratios (overall)	
4th (od)	2.88
3rd (high)	4.11
2nd	6.82
1st	12.1
R & T performance factor (high)	72.5

PERFORMANCE

Top speed, high gear	104.7
overdrive	102.1
Max. speeds in gears—	
2nd od (5600)	94
2nd (5600)	66
1st (5600)	37
Shift points from—	
2nd (5200)	61
1st (5200)	34
Mileage	18/22 mpg

ACCELERATION

0-30 mph	2.9 secs
0-40 mph	5.7 secs
0-50 mph	7.2 secs
0-60 mph	9.7 secs
0-70 mph	13.1 secs
0-80 mph	18.8 secs
0-90 mph	28.0 secs
Standing ¼ mile —	
average	17.4
best	17.2

TAPLEY READINGS

Gear	Lbs/ton		Mph
1st	off scale		—
2nd	580	at	44
3rd	385	at	52
od	250	at	60
Total drag at 60 mph, 154 lbs.			

SPEEDO ERROR

Indicated	Actual
10	12.1
20	19.5
30	28.9
40	38.0
50	47.7
60	57.4
70	67.0
80	76.2
90	86.5

Chevrolet V-8 Coupe
Acceleration through the gears

GM CONTRASTS-

BUICK and CHEVROLET

Now that they are both among

AN AUTO AGE STAFF REPORT

PHOTOS BY DAN RUBIN

ROAD
AUTO AGE
TEST

THERE IS A TENDENCY among auto testers to compare any new car with its immediate predecessor —that is, the last year's model of the same car. This is all well and good for the buyer who is determined to stick with one brand of auto through thick and thin but who is still interested in how his particular machine stacks up against the very latest model. However, one large factor is usually ignored completely: the huge majority of motorists are terribly interested in how one car stacks up against another one made by a different company, perhaps even in a different price range. There really is no such thing as a "low-priced" car any more and the buyer has a right to know just what he is paying for when it comes to a choice between two different cars.

With this in mind, we took for our tests two General Motors cars—the Buick and the Chevrolet—and put them through exactly the same paces to find the strong and weak points of each. This is not intended as a strict comparison or even as an indication of which is the better car; we feel that with so many varied uses and requirements for an automobile in this country there is almost no such thing as a "best" car, except as it pertains to a specific individual. And this is a changing, variable factor.

We chose as our test cars the Buick Riviera hardtop and the Chevy four-door V-8 Bel Air sedan, attempting to hit upon what we thought would probably turn out to be the most popular model in each line. First we looked for external appearance. Taken from a head-on view, the Chevrolet seems to have a definite edge over its big brother, mostly because of the beautiful simplicity of the in-slanted, rectangular-shaped, Italian-style grille and the direct, functional bumper. You may even prefer the

CONTINUED ON NEXT PAGE

Dash panel of the Buick Super, above, features a machined center strip upon which all instruments except speedometer are placed. Below, compact Chevrolet dash.

me "big three" in sales, Buick and Chevy have become rivals.   Here's how they rate.

Here the Buick and its little brother are seen negotiating the same corner on the AUTO AGE testing course. Buick looks comparatively flat because it has broken away; a moment later it spun completely.

On really tight turns the Buick tends to lean more than the Chevrolet due to its softer suspension, greater weight. Cars were both doing 30 mph.

simple rear-end treatment of the smaller car to the bold, heavily-chromed tail assembly of the Buick, but that is a delicate point. Viewed in profile, the Buick begins to take command, presenting a lower, longer, more sweeping line. Admittedly, this particular Buick is more of a sports model, but its styling is carried through on the bulkier sedans as well. The car not only looks longer, it is, by some 20 inches, and this adds to the feeling of luxury. Besides, the extra foot of wheelbase pays off in directional stability, making the Buick a better, smoother road car on long, fast, straight highways.

But there is a loss for every gain. Whereas the longer wheelbase helps the Buick in a straight line, it hinders it by comparison when there are corners to be taken. In our handling tests, the Chevrolet showed itself to be a much better cornering car than the Buick, so much so that it was able to get through turns at 30 mph that the Buick had trouble with at 25. Part of this, of course, was

the steering. The Chevy seems to have a bit more feel in the steering wheel and rather less of a tendency to oversteer though both wheels go 5¾ turns from lock to lock. The Buick's oversteer characteristic, combined with its additional weight—about 1,000 lbs. more—caused it to drift out more in turns, and it was more difficult to correct. Both cars, however, were remarkably resistant to roll-over and we were never able to come close to picking a wheel off the ground, even though the Buick spun around completely on one corner, attempting to go through at the same speed as the Chevy. As far as lean was concerned, the two cars seemed about equal on all but the sharpest turns where the Buick tilted a degree or so more than the smaller sedan. At no point did the angle of lean become alarming on either car. Perhaps the reason we were able to drive the Chevy through some of the turns somewhat flatter was the fact that its size permitted us to break it loose easier into a controlled

Virtually thrown into this corner, the Bel Air V-8 proved to have fine correction control, good stability. Note bent front tire.

In the braking tests the Buick's weight again stood in its way, causing it to slide more on panic stops. Both cars have fine brakes.

drift, and once a car starts to lose any traction in this manner, most of the lean disappears. Thus, a drift is used as a sort of safety valve.

The real reason for the Chevrolet's outstanding handling, of course—and for its improved ride, which almost equals that of the Buick—is the ball-joint front suspension which was borrowed from Ford, and which Ford borrowed from the British Jaguar. You have all read of the virtues of ball-joint suspension, so there is no point in going into any great detail here. What is important is that Chevrolet has it while no other General Motors car has been so equipped as yet. Thus, the little Chevy should outhandle them all. We predict that every car in the GM line will have this superior suspension—or its equivalent —by next year. It's just a shame that they didn't make it for '55.

There were some more interesting contrasts inside the cars. We were able to get the opinions of some relatively short—but charming—ladies on the matter of comparative seat comfort and visibility, and here is what they thought:

The Chevy, as it turned out, had the more advantageous seating position for a short person since it gave the most over-the-hood visibility in the extreme forward position. In addition, it actually came forward much closer to the pedals; the closest position on the Buick is still too far away for a woman less than five feet two inches tall. And in case you are wondering, men, why we are harping so much on the accessability of these cars for women, let's hear you deny that your wife does at least one-third of the driving in your family!

As for the rest of the interiors of the two cars, there is little to choose between them except that there is, of course, more hiproom on the Buick seats, as well as a few more luxury appointments. The Buick's foot-controlled parking brake is still a good feature in that it can be applied quickly and easily while riding if a real emergency arises.

When it comes to sheer power and acceleration, the Buick is not only far ahead of the Chevrolet—it is one of the fastest, most responsive cars in this country, regardless of price. With its new variable-pitch Dynaflow, especially starting in low, the Super zooms off like a jet fighter in one unbroken, silken-smooth sweep. It will

actually outrun many high-priced sports cars in a straight line. It will get from a dead start to 30 mph in 3.3 seconds in low and to 40 mph in 4.9. Zero to 60 mph, still in low range, took only 11.1 seconds. Running in drive range, these times were knocked off considerably, the car reaching 30 mph in 4.9 seconds, 40 in 6.7 seconds and 60 in 13.3 seconds, still plenty fast. Passing acceleration from 30 to 50 mph in drive range consumed 4.1 seconds.

The Chevrolet is somewhat slower than the Buick, but this is to be expected. Just figure out the power-to-weight ratios and you will see that the larger car has to be faster. Still, GM's little breadwinner is no slouch even in this department. Acceleration figured (*Continued on page 30*)

(*Continued on page 30*)

Buick's trunk is so tremendous that with the lid up it looks like a hungry whale. It can be employed to carry all the luggage for a family of nine or fitted out as a roomy sun porch as demonstrated above.

29

GM Contrasts—Buick and Chevrolet

to 4.6 seconds from zero to 30, 6.9 to 40 and 13.8 to 60 mph. These were the best times we got with the car, using both low and drive range. Passing acceleration here from 30 to 50 mph came to 5.4 seconds.

In the top speed departments, the Chevrolet hit about 101 mph and the Buick roared up to 108, but it got there a lot faster because after 70 mph it really begins to move while the Chevy starts to flatten out just a little past that point.

Both cars were equipped with power brakes and while we didn't actually measure stopping distance in our tests, it was obvious from the start that the Chevrolet could be brought down to a dead stop in fewer feet than the Buick every time. Here again weight was the major factor, with the lighter car's superior front suspension again getting an assist because of its ability to cut down on weight transfer and nosedive during hard deceleration. Out on the highway, the braking story was somewhat different; that is to say both cars performed about equally in slowing the car from 60 mph, for instance, down to 20. Obviously, when the brakes weren't

slammed on as they might be in an emergency, the weight factor became less important.

We were talking earlier about gain and loss. We know that the Buick is a more powerful car than the Chevrolet. The loss in this connection is in the matter of gasoline mileage. Our test Chevrolet consumed gas at a rate of some 16.4 miles to the gallon. This was on a brand new car with less than 2,000 miles on the clock. The Buick, on the other hand, got only a little over 11 miles per gallon under the same conditions, and since it is running a 9-to-1 compression ratio, every gallon you pour into that huge tank had better be high-test gas. Actually, we were running the Buick pretty hard and we had it in low range much of the time, so ordinary city mileage should run over 13 miles per gallon and it will probably stretch to 17 or 19 on the open road. As for the Chevy, it will get at least 16 miles per gallon in the city and anywhere from 18 to 23 on the pike. It's all a matter of what kind of driving you do most of the time.

And that, in fact, is the real point in chosing between the two cars. If you do a lot of city driving, or make hundreds of short hops over back roads that wind in and out like Marilyn Monroe's profile, then the Chevy is probably the better car for you. But if you have more highway traveling to do, and make a habit of covering 500 or 600 miles at a clip, the Buick is your meat, by all means. As we said, there is no such thing as a "better" car.

In our evaluation of these two cars, we have, to this point, avoided all mention of price. This would, at first glance, seem to be the logical proceedure in view of the fact that the Buick and Chevrolet are in two separate price ranges and it would be reasonable to assume, therefore, that they would appeal to entirely different audiences. For years the Chevy has been the largest-selling automobile in the U. S.—challenged now by Ford for that leadership—with Plymouth assumed to be the third member of the "Big Three." But towards the end of 1954, Buick sales catapulted so high that they displaced Plymouth as the third largest seller, thus joining Chevy in the charmed triangle.

What does this indicate? Well, it would seem that there is a growing segment of American motorists who can afford at least $3,000 for a car and who choose their machines on the basis of performance, looks and utility rather than on a strict dollar scale. Accordingly, the Buick and Chevrolet have suddenly become hot competitors. If you are in the market for a new car, and price—within reason—is of secondary importance, you would do well to look into the Buick and Chevrolet. They are both fine automobiles. ●

BUICK SPECIFICATIONS

ENGINE: V-8, overhead valves; bore 4.00 in.; stroke, 3.20 in.; total displacement, 322 cu. in.; developed hp, 236 at 4,600 rpm; torque, 330 lb./ft. at 3,000 rpm; compression ratio, 9 to 1; single four-barrel down-draft carburetor; mechanical fuel pump; crankcase capacity, 6 qts.; radiator capacity, 18 qts.; ignition, 12 volts.

TRANSMISSION: Dynaflow torque convertor with variable pitch stator blades.

REAR AXLE RATIO: 3.40 to 1 standard; 3.90 to 1 optional.

SUSPENSION: independent, by coils and hydraulic shock absorbers.

BRAKES: four-wheel hydraulic with power booster and vacuum reserve tank.

DIMENSIONS: wheelbase, 127 in.; front tread, 62.2 in.; width, 80 in.; height, 62.6 in.; over-all length, 216 in.; turning circle, 43 ft.; ground clearance, 6.6 in.; dry weight, 4,075 lbs.; tires, 7.60 x 15, tubeless.

PERFORMANCE

ACCELERATION: Zero to 30 mph: 3.3 seconds
Zero to 40 mph: 4.9 seconds
Zero to 60 mph: 11.1 seconds
TOP SPEED: 108 mph

CHEVROLET SPECIFICATIONS

ENGINE: V-8, overhead valves; bore 3.75 in.; stroke, 3.00 in.; total displacement, 265 cu. in.; developed hp, 162 at 4,400 rpm (power kit available to raise hp to 180 at 4,600 mph); torque, 257 lb./ft. at 2,200 rpm; compression ratio, 8 to 1; single two-barrel down-draft carburetor; mechanical fuel pump; crankcase capacity, 4 qts.; radiator capacity, 17 qts.; ignition, 12 volts.

TRANSMISSION: Powerglide torque converter.

REAR AXLE RATIO: 3.55 to 1 standard; 3.70 and 4.11 available.

SUSPENSION: front by individual coils and hydraulic shock absorbers; rear by semi-elliptic leaf springs and hydraulic shock absorbers.

BRAKES: four-wheel hydraulic with power booster and vacuum reserve tank.

DIMENSIONS: wheelbase, 115 in.; front tread, 58 in.; rear tread, 58.8 in.; width, 74 in.; height, 62.1 in.; over-all length, 195.6 in.; turning circle, 38 ft.; ground clearance, 6.5 in.; dry weight, 3,190 lbs.; tires, 6.70 x 15 tubeless.

PERFORMANCE

ACCELERATION: Zero to 30 mph: 4.6 seconds
Zero to 40 mph: 6.9 seconds
Zero to 60 mph: 13.8 seconds
TOP SPEED: 101 mph

CHEVROLET'S NEW V-8

(Continued from page 17)

to the sump through passages drilled in the heads and block.

Now you tell me how you're going to put together a V-8 engine at less cost than Chevrolet has put this one together!

WILL IT STAND UP?

Chevrolet has never yet put out an engine that *didn't* stand up. But everything on the new design is so ridiculously simple and straightforward that you can't help but wonder if the thing will stay month after month, winter and summer, with the more elaborate V-8s. The whole thing is so simple that there's almost *got* to be a catch somewhere! If the new Chevy engine *does* hang in with the other V-8s, what use will there be anymore to cast or forge rocker arms, machine rocker shafts, spend time and money carefully machining pushrod ends and sockets, use floating piston pins, etc.?

Actually, this is a tough one to answer on paper. These rocker ball joints are entirely new and untried; offhand, they look like they could get sloppy pretty quick . . . but who knows? Up to now pushrod ends and seats (sockets) have been a critical point. Can Chevy get away with simple crimping and stamped seats, even with their more ample lubrication?

Their engineers, backed by thousands of miles of road tests, must figure the setup will take it in everyday operation or they wouldn't be putting it on the road. But then, the Ford engineers thought their '54 camshaft would take it, too . . . and the lab boys said that Buick's original V-8 combustion chamber wouldn't knock too badly at 8½:1 compression! Only time will tell the Chevy story.

On the other hand, the design shows many good features aimed specifically at long life. Precision insert bearings of G.M. Durex (copper-nickel matrix with thin babbitt overlay) are used for rods and mains. These babies are tough. Also, they don't groove and lower half of the main shells, which is said to increase their load-carrying capacity 40%. The oil control piston ring is of the very efficient steel rail type, chrome plated for durability. These will control oil consumption even with considerable bore wear, when old-style rings would be burning a quart of oil every 50 miles. A new aluminum dip process that has been found to reduce exhaust valve oxidation (burning) is featured. Couple all this with the very short stroke, low piston travel, compact, rigid block, good stud layout around the cylinders . . . and certainly the new Chevy V-8 is going to have a fighting chance to live as long as the more expensive mills in our industry.

HIGH PERFORMANCE PACKAGE

For the first time in their ultra-conservative history, Chevrolet is letting the hair down and offering you a little extra oomph for the family chariot right at your corner dealership. The 1955 "high performance package" for the V-8 includes a 4 barrel carburetor, matching large-port intake manifold, and dual exhaust system. Advertised rated output for the combo is 180 hp at 4600 rpm, and 260 lb.-ft. torque at 2800. (Output as installed in the car is stated to be 160 hp.) I'm thinking a little, light Chev ought to really jump with this stuff under the hood!

In conclusion on Chevy's new V-8: It's definitely a highly advanced and progressive design, but mostly from the standpoint of manufacturing economics rather than performance and general functional efficiency. You'll never build a modern V-8 engine at less cost than they're building this one. But at the same time, I think it has plenty of port and valve area, combustion control, and mechanical efficiency (low friction loss) to stay with the competition very nicely in the horsepower race. The engine is also very compact and light. The only doubts I would have are in regard to the durability of the valve gear. Since it's an entirely new layout, only time will tell. •

CHEVROLET ROAD TEST

(Continued from page 15)

dow means soaked upholstery and a closed window means slow suffocation or steamy glass areas.

Seats are deep, soft and comfortable and upholstery fabrics, in the more expensive models, are top quality woolens, nylons and leatherettes in many shades and colors, all designed to complement the car's exterior paint job. Optional extra for the car this year includes electric windshield wipers for those who dislike waiting for a vacuum buildup. Electrical system is twelve volt, showing an industry-wide move toward the larger capacity system.

Chevrolet for 1955, like so many of the more expensive cars, has also gone to tubeless tires. The MOTOR *Life* test staff found these tires completely satisfactory as compared with the conventional inner tube and tire. Although perfected to a point where they will probably never break the air seal, tubeless tires or too-low pressure seemed to be at fault for the only minor annoyances we found in the Chevrolet's handling, steering and cornering. Tubeless tires, in the main, are puncture and blow-out proof. With this guaranteed insurance, the American mo-

torist can soon start leaving his spare tire at home. This procedure would not only add more luggage space to his car, but would decrease the car's weight by about 50 pounds—poundage which can make a difference in acceleration.

Summed up, the Chevrolet for 1955 is a gathering together of the best mechanical and design features available in the industry today. It now has a V-8, ball-joint suspension, a big car look, and even paint treatments which resemble the big cars. To Americans who have always liked GM's psychology that the Chevrolet is just a small Olds, this year's model will go a long way toward carrying that belief toward full fruition.

Whether Chevrolet's gamble on this close resemblance between its car and the Oldsmobile will help Chevy sales or harm Olds sales remains to be seen. The Chevrolet Bel Air or convertible with the "power package" plus its natural lines would seem to be a better buy for the same money than one of the older brothers in a sedan model, with more horsepower—but a lot more weight.

With their primary target a dominant first in sales again—Chevrolet enters the new model year better-equipped for out-and-out comparison than it has ever been. •

1956 chevrolet

HIGHLIGHTS: top of 205 hp, front end with a tilt, new four-door hardtop and nine-passenger station wagon and shoulder harness seat belts

CHEVROLET plans to keep its remarkable reputation for outstanding performance going strong in 1956. With this in mind, engines ratings of up to 205 horsepower are being offered buyers for the coming year. Styling hasn't been forgotten either; although the basic body shell—new in 1955—remains the same, detail changes have been made to increase the car's already broad appeal and several new body types have been created to fill out the line.

One of the more interesting things about the increased horsepower ratings of the engines is that they have been made with no increase in displacement. The Super Turbo-Fire V-8, which now puts out the 205 horsepower, remains at 265 cubic inches. The boost comes from a new high-lift camshaft, compression ratio of 9.25-to-1 and other detail refinements. A four-barrel carbureter is standard on this engine.

Two other V-8 engines are also available: one installed in standard shift cars and the other standard on Powerglide models. The first continues at 162 horsepower, same as 1955, while the standard Powerglide engine is rated at 170 horsepower. All V-8 engines used in 1956 Chevrolets will have hydraulic valve lifters, with solid lifters optional.

The promise of outstanding performance in Chevrolet's 205-horsepower engine already has been demonstrated. A record-breaking run up Pikes Peak by a heavily disguised 1956 Chevrolet clipped more than two minutes from the former standard passenger car record for this run.

A pre-production '56 camouflaged with plastic hoods and a weird paint job made the 12.42-mile climb in 17 minutes, 24:05 seconds. The old record was 19 minutes, 25:70 seconds and had stood for 21 years.

The car was driven by Zora Arkus-Duntov, a Chevrolet engineer, and was certified by NASCAR. NASCAR officials timed the run, certified the car as stock after tearing the engine down and checking it against 1956 specifications.

Among witnesses at the run were Bill France, NASCAR president, and "Cannonball" Baker, former holder of the stock car record for the climb.

A good test of a car's roadability and handling, as well as its power and acceleration, the road up Pikes Peak climbs thru a series of 170 sharp turns and cut-backs to the summit, 14,110 feet above sea level.

Chevrolet's traditional valve-in-head six has been retained for customers who prefer it to the V-8. Modifications including higher lift cam, new al-dipped exhaust valves and compression ratio of 8-to-1 have raised horsepower to 140, however. At the same time, better gasoline mileage is claimed. Hydraulic valve lifters are used in the six also.

Major styling change involves the grille. Chevrolet introduced a remarkably clean-looking arrangement last year and, while it was a hit with most enthusiasts, the company's buyer research apparently indicated that a more massive appearance was desired by a majority of the car

Styling highlights of 1956 Chevrolets are represented in the three photos here. Forward cant of the front end has been emphasized by stretching the hood metal out another four inches. This, with angled headlight hoods and grille, give illusion of motion. Car at top is Bel Air convertible, center is standard sedan, while new sport sedan is at the bottom.

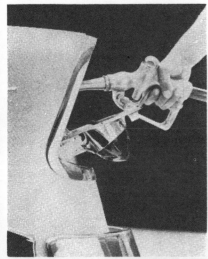

Cleaner lines (left, top and bottom) results from hiding gas intake in Buick-like taillights. Note wheel baffles above.

Instrument panel changes are few for '56. Chevrolet now offers seat belts with shoulder harness as optional equipment.

Massive frontal treatment is rather drastic change from much simpler treatment in 1955 front ends. Car has longer look.

Chevy V-8 in its first year unquestionably became the new favorite among enthusiasts. Top rating for 1956 is 205 hp.

buyers. Therefore, although the lattice-work effect remains, the grille has been widened and parking lights have been enlarged, becoming almost integral with the grille. Plane of the hood has been flattened and extends four inches farther forward before dipping to meet the grille. This, along with higher, straighter front and rear fender lines, gives the illusion of greater length.

Chrome body moldings have been re-designed and this type of treatment has been extended to the lowest-priced 150 series for the first time. These moldings, in keeping with current practice, serve as natural division points for two-tone paint treatments.

Chevrolet now offers 19 different body styles—more variety than ever before. One of the new models, as was expected, is a four-door hardtop. Also introduced for the first time is a nine-passenger station wagon.

The company has jumped on the safety bandwagon. In fact, in the matter of

CONTINUED ON PAGE 38

driving the 1956 chevrolet

THE 1956 Chevrolet has already proved itself by breaking the stock car record for the Pikes Peak climb—in a time only about three minutes over the current race car record. I drove the same heavily-disguised four-door hardtop which set the record and was very impressed by its performance and handling. The 205-hp engine makes top speed and acceleration excellent and the car has a responsive, very stable feel.

Maurie Rose turned the wheel over to me after giving me a fast tour of the varied roads and high-speed track at GM's proving grounds. After a few familiarization runs, we made a few quick performance checks using fifth wheel and two stop watches. Although the car was handicapped by the clutch—the heavy-duty one standard with the 205-hp engine

was badly worn after practice and record runs at the Peak and had been replaced by a standard unit—acceleration was good. Zero to 60 mph took 12 seconds flat and 50 to 70 about 6.9 seconds. With the heavier clutch which would make faster starts possible, the 0-60 time could have been cut noticeably, I'm sure.

Braking was very positive, though a little sudden due to dirt in the drums from the Peak runs. Chevrolet's anti-dive feature introduced last year is one of the things that makes driving the car very enjoyable.

This car had been driven very hard, as you can imagine, at Pikes Peak; many practice runs were made before the official record-breaker. Despite that, it performed nobly and was really a lot of fun to drive.

—Ken Fermoyle

Improved Handling in

Ball-joint front end, new steering box did the trick, reports Bryan Hanrahan

TEN more horses, ball-joint front end and a new wrinkle in the contour distinguish our Chevrolet for 1956—a fast, vast, elegant and roadworthy motor-car.

Power plant is still the straight-six o.h.v. engine (the few V8's in the country being privately imported)—but this, I found, is nothing to moan about.

With average load, the torque produced by its 120 developed horsepower will leave a swathe of smoking rubber on the road if handled clumsily.

All of which reminds me that the standard Chevrolet sedan, with V8 motor and manual gearshift, is reported to be beating all comers in the popular U.S. form of stock-car racing — the mass-start standing quarter-mile.

Many Improvements

For 1956 the Chev's designers seem to have concentrated on making the car more roadable.

Breathing of the engine has been improved to produce the extra power. The performance table shows acceleration to be 8 to 10 percent better all round than figures put up by the previous model. With the 7.1 to 1 compression, however, the introduction of premium fuel since my last test must account for some of the gain.

Maximum speed, a genuine 95 m.p.h., is about 2 m.p.h. better, and

the overall fuel figure of 19.2 m.p.g. over a relatively short test of 118 miles, including punching into a strong head-wind, is remarkably good.

But the most valuable improvements, I found, are in the steering and front end. Deplorably low-geared for a fast car at 5¼ turns lock to lock, the wheel can nevertheless be manipulated by one finger right down to 6-7 m.p.h. I put this down to the new recirculating ball and sector-type steering box, noted for its lightness of action.

The incredibly good turning circle (35½ft.) removes one of the curses of a large car in heavy traffic. Find 20 feet of clear space at the kerb, and the near-17 feet of Chevrolet can be manoeuvred in without effort, although the wheel-winding may make you a little giddy.

At speed the steering gives a reassuring feeling of close acquaintance with the road surface. Reaction in the hands is slight, except on rough stuff. The wheel kicks but does not jar.

We Hit the Dirt

An evil eye was cast about for some really horrid dirt surfaces to try out the new ball-joint front end. Melbourne being what it is, exactly

what was required was found in the inner suburbs—there was nothing comparable in our speed-testing area 30 miles from town.

At this stage of operations I had got the hang of the car through fast bends on smooth bitumen. The usual considerations of length and weight borne in mind, performance was quite good. Roll was pronounced, but wheel-grip tenacious and tyre noise low.

The steering characteristics are first-class for entering a bend, but response to correction is slow if one tends to overdo it a bit.

Boring-in with the stops out required more skill than I was able to acquire during the rather short test run. Even so, the exceptional lightness of the steering made it possible to take the Chev over the horror stretch as fast as wheel adhesion would allow: a little anticipation and a quick spin of the wheel was all that was necessary. Here the front end was quite outstanding. It ironed out uneven surfaces and ran faithfully to line.

The other end, with nothing in the rear seat or boot, was not so happy. Axle hop (as distinct from loss of adhesion through applying too much power) and plunging were induced over the rough going.

Much as I enjoyed putting this big saloon through its paces, my passenger rolled about on the huge front seat like a pea on a drum. There is no lateral support for the occupants other than the driver—who must hang on to the large, high-set steering wheel.

The combination of soft suspension and bench seats demands at least central armrests in such a fast car. Their absence spoils the fun of a motorist who likes on occasions to really drive his car with passengers aboard. Light and easy control of the wheel is denied him, moreover.

A Suggestion

I would like to see this Chev fitted with ride control, which I think is essential to the large and very fast American cars now in production.

56 Chev

Only one of the big manufacturers has it at present, yet it seems the logical complement to increased performance potential. It follows the usual pattern of systems used on many big and heavy Continental cars, whereby the flick of a switch instantly hardens the suspension for fast cruising or cornering. In normal city-suburban driving conditions another flick brings back that soft, easy glide.

For several years many American cars have been capable of being driven beyond the safe limits of the soft suspension demanded by the average buyer. But such safety devices as dished steering wheels, crash-pads, and stronger door-locks—all very well in their way—cannot replace balanced design characteristics. What is the point in having this extra power unless it can be used to the full?

I am no advocate of scorching around everywhere; as a man who loves driving, I just like to get my full money's worth out of my car when road conditions allow me to indulge in a little fast work.

What a fate to be a busy commercial traveller who must cover long distances in a car with power to burn, but without the roadworthiness to make full use of it!

Mechanically, the Chevrolet's front suspension, with self-adjusting ball-joints, is much better than the conventional layout. The bearing points

(Continued on page 38)

DASH has a fan-shaped instrument panel, balanced on passenger's side by a radio grille. Visibility through the windscreen is excellent.

STRAIGHT SIX engine now breathes better, churns out 120 b.h.p. Performance is 8 to 10 percent better all round than previous models

SPECIFICATIONS

ENGINE: 6-cylinder, o.h.v.; bore 3 9-16in., stroke 3 15-16in., capacity 235 cu. in.; compression ratio 7.1 to 1; R.A.C. rating 30.4 h.p., maximum b.h.p. 120 at 3800 r.p.m.; weight to power ratio 27.5lb. b.h.p.; downdraught carburettor; mechanical fuel pump; ignition, 12v.
TRANSMISSION: Diaphragm spring type clutch; synchromesh on all gears; hypoid bevel final drive; back axle ratio 3.1 to 1.
SUSPENSION: Front, independent coil and stabiliser; rear, semi-elliptics; hydraulic double-acting shock absorbers.
BRAKES: Hydraulic, self-energising.
STEERING: Ball-bearing roller sector, turning circle 35ft. 6in.; 5¼ turns lock-to-lock.
DIMENSIONS: Wheelbase 9ft. 7in., length 16ft. 10in., width 6ft. 4in., height 5ft. 5in.; clearance 8in.; track, front, 4ft. 8 11-16in., rear. 4ft. 10¾in.
WEIGHT: 30 cwt. (kerb).
FUEL TANK: 13 1-3rd gallons.

PERFORMANCE

CONDITIONS: Strong headwind, dry tarmac, two occupants, premium fuel
MAXIMUM SPEED: 96 m.p.h.
STANDING quarter-mile: 19.9sec.
FLYING quarter-mile: 95.1 m.p.h.
MAXIMUM speeds in gears: First, 32 m.p.h.; second, 66; third, 96.
ACCELERATION through gears: 0-30, 5.1s.; 0-40, 8.6s.; 0-50, 10.8s.; 0-60, 18.1s.; 0-70, 25.9s.
ACCELERATION in 2nd gear: 10-30, 5.1s.; 20-40, 5.3s.; 30-50, 6.1s.; 40-60, 9s.
ACCELERATION in top gear: 10-30, 8s.; 20-40, 8.2.; 30-50, 9.3s.; 40-60, 9.7s.; 50-70, 10.8s.
PULLING POWER (Tapley readings): First gear, 620lb. per ton, gradient 1 in 3.9; second, 490, 1 in 4.6; top (max.), 305, 1 in 7 (equals 48 m.p.h.); retard rate at 30 m.p.h., 42lb.
BRAKE EFFICIENCY (Tapley readings): Footbrake from 30 m.p.h., 92 percent; fade test, 89 percent; handbrake equal to 1 in 3.8 grade.
BRAKING: 30 m.p.h. to stop—36ft. 10in.
FUEL CONSUMPTION: 19.2 m.p.g. (including all tests).
SPEEDOMETER: 3 percent slow at 30 m.p.h., 4 percent fast at 60, 6 percent fast at 90.

(All acceleration and speed figures are averages of two runs each way in opposite directions.)

PRICE: £1681 with tax

1956 chevrolet

FOR 1956, Chevrolet has taken a well-designed, successful car and made worthwhile improvements in appearance, performance, and comfort. People who liked the car in 1955 will like it even more so this year, and for the same basic reasons. Noteworthy improvements have been made in noise reduction and the smoothing out of vibration caused by minor irregularities in road surface.

Body structure is very solidly assembled; there are no squeaks or rattles in windshield, doors or windows. CAR LIFE's test car was a 4-door hardtop with the greatest expanse of unbraced bodywork from front to rear. Wrap-around windshield no longer squeaks or chirps as it did on most '55 models.

The car is unusually quiet-running. Powerglide has lost the characteristic whine found in so many Chevvies of previous years. V8 engine is remarkably quiet and smooth even when the kickdown into Low range is activated. This kickdown can be made only up to about 55 mph; for acceleration from there on up there is only the torque converter and the power of the engine. With Powerglide transmission when hill-climbing or accelerating, plenty of power is needed, and the 205-bhp power pack (dual carburetor etc.), would be advisable for competing with the performance of two other low-priced cars with their standard V8 equipment.

Chevrolet's high card, this year as last, is its controllability and roadability. The combination of a well-balanced chassis and the ball-joint front suspension is almost perfect. Even with power steering, there is almost perfect "road feel," and this still holds even on slippery or icy going.

Roadability is the best in the price class at average cruising speeds of 50-60 mph on crowned, rolling and uneven-surfaced roads. There is no mushy dive into turns when you start to crank the wheel sharply . . . there is little or no body roll. Power steering sometimes seems to give a sensation like oversteer, but this has not been evidenced on non-power steering '55 cars.

The Chevvy's ride is well controlled but not as soft or vibration-free as one competitor in the same price group. There has been a calculated engineering choice in favor of roadability and secure control at the expense of a soft suspension that could blot up small bumps and vibration.

The ride is as good, perhaps even better as far as absorbing of surface vibration is concerned, than on a couple of more expensive cars with greater weights and longer wheelbases. Recovery out of sharp dips is excellent and rebound is well controlled. The two-barreled, 170-bhp version of the Chevvy engine ran butter-smooth and responded quickly to the throttle. Gasoline economy, using regular grade fuel, is not exceptional, especially if there is considerable acceleration and deceleration, hill climbing, etc.

It would be advisable for any Chevvy buyer to try a car without power steering before spending the extra 85 dollars. The recirculating ball, worm-and-block system permits smooth, easy steering. Only if almost all of the driving is to be done in tight, city traffic would we recommend power steering.

Power brakes, however, are a different matter. With the new cars growing heavier each year, power brakes are a

BEL AIR HARDTOP

definite aid to driving ease.

Seats are comfortable and the padding has been thoughtfully beefed-up to give added support to the base of the spine, where it's needed on long drives. Sound proofing is excellent; both road and engine noise are well muffled. With all windows and ventilator panes shut tight there is almost no wind roar even at 70 mph and over.

Body shakes and vibration have been cut down. Cobblestone and car tracks, expansion joints, etc., are scarcely felt, and the frame gives a very solid feel. Body insulators seem to soak up the vibration without giving a soft or rubbery feel.

Interiors are comfortable and colorful (on Bel Air series) but the finishing and assembly left some distinctly rough edges. Windows cranked extremely stiffly, even for a new car. However, it should be considered that the test car was a 4-door hardtop, new to Chevrolet this year.

The rattle-free, draft-free condition of this four-door hard top is distinctly a feather in the cap of Fisher Body Division of GM. They have set a high standard for this model that the other two automotive giants will do well to live up to.

Summing up: A solidly built car with exceptional roadability and all-around handling ease. Buyers have a choice of the time-tested, dependable six-cylinder engine that gives only ordinary performance with the automatic transmission, or a well-designed, short-stroke V8 with extremely smooth, quiet and powerful performance (but medium to low gas mileage), with the automatic transmission. ●

YOUR CHECK LIST

☑ ☑ ☑ ☑ ☑ means top rating

PERFORMANCE ☑ ☑ ☑ ☑ ☐
Brisk and lively with 170 bhp V8 and Powerglide. Chevrolet, although it exceeds the competition in its price class with the 205-bhp, 4-barrel carburetor powerpack, offers only 162 bhp on the standard price V8 with manual transmission.

STYLING ☑ ☑ ☑ ☑ ☐
A tastefully revamped version of General Motors squarish, easy-to-live-with styling. The two-tone side panel effects on Bel Air models are a bit cluttered, but the different treatment of "210" model panels (two-toned for the first time this year) is excellent.

RIDING COMFORT ☑ ☑ ☑ ☑ ☐
Chevrolet's ride makes an excellent compromise between the ultra-soft cushioned suspension (where stability is sacrificed), and the other extreme of too-hard springing. There is almost complete freedom from roll, swaying or pitching. Surface vibrations are still felt, but are less noticeable than in '55 cars.

INTERIOR DESIGN ☑ ☑ ☑ ☑ ☐
Forward vision, relative location of seat, steering wheel and foot controls are good. Arm rests are a bit too low for maximum driver comfort. Seats give better than average support to the lower back, and are very comfortable for long drives.

ROADABILITY ☑ ☑ ☑ ☑ ☑
Tops in its field. Driver has almost perfect "road sense" at all times. Excellent balance between understeer and oversteer. Car tracks perfectly even in rough going or with strong cross wind. Responds instantly to steering correction. Car does not sway or "nose dive," has minimum amount of roll.

EASE OF CONTROL ☑ ☑ ☑ ☑ ☐
Generally good, although brakes minus power assist take more pedal pressure than other light cars. The recirculating ball steering needs no power assist. Shifting Powerglide transmission into Low range gives good braking on hills.

ECONOMY ☑ ☑ ☑ ☑ ☐
Only fair on 170 bhp V8 with Powerglide transmission. Can be improved noticeably if car is driven with a light foot. Combination of V8 and overdrive transmission should give mileage close to the best.

SERVICEABILITY ☑ ☑ ☑ ☑ ☐
Very good, even with power accessories. Chassis is simple and well designed, with minimum of greasing points. Spark plugs, in an awkward position below the exhaust manifold, are the only tricky item.

WORKMANSHIP ☑ ☑ ☑ ☑ ☐
Average for the price class. Metal finishing, fit of panels and paint job are good. Interior trim, upholstery, etc., showed some rough edges. However, there were no rattles on the test car.

DURABILITY ☑ ☑ ☑ ☑ ☐
Fisher bodies, used on all GM cars, have a well-founded reputation for holding up. Chevvy chassis is simple and rugged. The new V8 engine is extremely well-designed and sturdy.

VALUE PER DOLLAR ☑ ☑ ☑ ☑ ☑
Ties with the other sales volume leader for the best transportation investment in both its field and the industry. Depreciation is nearly the lowest and repairs are infrequent.

CONTINUED FROM PAGE 33

restraining devices it has gone the rest of the industry one better, offering not only seat belts but shoulder harnesses, too! This is just a bit surprising because Chevrolet in the past seemed to feel that these items had little future in the passenger car. The value of safety belts was not questioned so much as the number of people who would actually use them. Could be that this is still the private belief of many, but at least they are now available. Crash-tested, positive-locking door latches and precision headlight aiming devices are two other items claimed to contribute to safety.

In what might be an attempt to appease dealers—those handling all makes screamed over the almost unlimited variety of colors and trims available in 1955—a "standard" two tone trim has been adopted for interiors of each series. "A wide range" of other harmonizing interiors will be optional, however.

Tail light treatment has been changed and '56 Chevrolets will have a distinctly Buick-like appearance from the rear. Gas filler caps are now concealed by hinged left rear tail lights instead of being under hinged flaps in the fender. This permits a smooth fender surface.

Here are the body styles available: 150 Series—two and four-door sedans, utility sedan and two-door, six-passenger station wagon; 210 Series—two and four-door sedans, Delray coupe, sport coupe and sedan, two and four-door six-passenger wagon and four-door, nine-passenger wagon; Bel Air Series—two and four-door sedans, sport coupe and sport sedan (hardtops), convertible, Nomad station wagon and four-door, nine-passenger wagon.

The 140-horsepower six-cylinder engine mentioned above will be the only six offered, incidentally. (Last year there were two. It will be used with both automatic and manual transmissions.

Optional items available will be full-flow oil filters, power steering, power brakes, push-button power seats and windows, air conditioning, tinted glass, etc.

Cited by Chevrolet as mechanical improvements are redesigned rear engine mounts (for better isolation of noise and vibration), electric water temperature gages replacing the old tube-type, improved batteries (carrying 36 instead of 21 month guarantees) and spark plugs and woven asbestos composition clutch facings for V-8 clutches. A high-capacity clutch of coil spring design is used instead of diaphragm spring clutches on 205-horsepower models.

Just as predicted in MOTOR LIFE's Forecast for '56 (September 1955) Chevrolet has followed a process of evolution in its 1956 models, not surprising in view of the extensive changes made last year. The result is a car that should uphold Chevrolet's tradition as a top seller. ●

CONTINUED FROM PAGE 35

are wide apart and automatically compensate for a degree of wear which would mean overhaul of king-pins and bushes.

Voltage Is Up

The other important change in this Chevrolet is the switch from 6-volt to 12-volt electrical system.

There are several reasons for it. The higher electrical pressure makes for smoother running of high-compression engines; more "pressure" is available for such auxiliaries as heaters, fans and radios; and contacts are less susceptible to the ravages of rust and dirt.

And, certainly, this classical straight-six power unit is as smooth as one could wish. It will sustain maximum revs without a trace of fuss or undue noise. No protest is heard at a pick-up from 6 m.p.h. in top gear. The engine is quiet and apparently effortless right up to the onset of valve bounce in the two lower ratios.

Controls, Instruments

The steering-column gearshift suffers from the usual long lever travel—a pity, because the fast synchromesh on all three forward ratios is a perfect match with the engine. Noise level in the indirect ratios is low.

Clutch is smooth, and transmits the surging engine torque with very little slip. The pendant pedal took some getting used to: the action is unexpectedly light, and the return spring seems to hesitate before asserting itself. For the first few miles I could not co-ordinate gear changes.

The organ-type throttle pedal is set rather high on the toeboard and also needs familiarity before a restful foot action can be achieved.

Brake pedal needs firm treatment, but the result is most gratifying at all times. The big car responds to braking from speed without any attempt to deviate from line. Some fade can be induced, but it is not serious.

Actually the foot controls are so positioned in relation to the toeboard that one must sharply bend the knees to operate them, with consequent loss of leverage. Their lightness does not altogether compensate. Perhaps this is why the wheel is so high-set, to clear the knees. I should imagine the top of the rim will interfere with a short driver's line of sight.

The handbrake, of the twist-and-pull variety, functions adequately if a hearty tug is applied.

One or two of the minor controls seem to assume ape-like proportions in the driver; in the conversion to right-hand drive they have not been shifted with the main functionaries—a minor but not especially praiseworthy economy.

Water-temperature gauge, speedometer (no trip recorder), and fuel gauge—but only warning lights for oil pressure and battery charge. Economy again?

The ignition lock, a hand-switch with key, needs a second movement of the key to lock it. The key can be removed with the switch left unlocked—a turn to the right and the engine starts, so don't "give" the car away.

Inside and Out

So far as interior sprawl room and seat comfort are concerned, there are bags and to spare; plenty of ashtrays, a cigar lighter, and a large illuminated glovebox. A little more of the space might, however, have been devoted to the driver's needs—and there is that lack of lateral support already mentioned.

Ventilation, by scuttle vent, admits plenty of air but no exhaust fumes from other traffic.

Vision all round, with wraparound glass front and rear, is excellent; both wings can be seen. The windscreen is not merely extended forward from the normal pillar line, leaving the same old blind spots.

Body lines are clean and happily free of confusing and superfluous ornament. The waist moulding will create no rust—it's stainless steel. Bumpers, well wrapped around front and rear, might acquit themselves well in a duel with a tank.

The Boot (capital B) could, I swear, take half a dozen sprawling occupants from the interior, despite the side-mounted spare wheel.

Despite my generalisations on the products of the American motor industry, I thought the Chev, as an example of it, a pretty wonderful piece of work. It has many endearing characteristics, and you get an awful lot of rugged, roomy and exciting car for your money. ●●●

How "HOT" is the CHEVROLET?

On straightaway runs and around closed circuits it takes power and control to stay out in front. And the Chevrolet V-8 has what it takes

Performance and styling are the two most popular yardsticks for measuring the worth of an automobile. Both are often the basis for spirited debate. But where styling involves a number of intangibles, performance is a matter of rather specific facts in the form of figures. This makes the job of evaluating the Chevrolet V-8's remarkable reputation easier. On this and the following five pages you will find (1) a brief resume of the car's competition record, (2) a road test (3) a technical analysis and (4) a look at what is available in the line for 1956.

THE 1955 Chevrolet was unquestionably the hottest volume production car on the nation's race tracks. It showed up best in NASCAR's short track division where it cinched the title by flattening all opposition. The box score gave it roughly three times as many victories and 10 times as many second places as its closest competition (which happened to be a car in a higher priced bracket). And current evidence indicates that the 1956 version of the quick V-8 has been substantially improved.

Even more precise information is reported by C. J. Hart, who runs the acceleration strip on the Orange County airport at Santa Ana, Calif., where proud non-professional owners flock on Sundays to match their car in supervised safety against their neighbors. Hart is unsurpassed as a qualified expert; week in and week out for more than five years he has stood at the starting line of the oldest and most active drag strip and watched the tireless amateurs race for the clocks a quarter-mile away.

The Chevrolet, according to Hart, is beyond a doubt the fastest stock car at Santa Ana. This, naturally, has caused its popularity to zoom and he estimates that the number of Chevrolets running has tripled over a year ago. It has easily become the new favorite of the enthusiast.

As this is written, the 1956 Chevrolet with standard transmission holds the stock record at 86.20 mph, the speed at which it passes the clocks after the quarter-mile of acceleration. For comparison, Hart reports that the next ranking 1956 cars, with the same type of gear boxes, are Buick Century at 85 mph and Ford at 84.74.

Hart figures out that the 1956 Chevrolet is a good 1½ mph faster than the 1955 with a stick shift and about one mph faster for the Powerglides, which now turn 81 mph in the standing quarter.

One final and significant observation from Hart cannot be omitted. He says that far fewer Chevrolets are blowing up from the strain of high rpm operation than last year. This indicates that the Flint engineers have somehow wrought the miracle of power with durability.

CONTINUED ON NEXT PAGE

TWO DIFFERENT 1956 Chevrolet V-8's were involved in this road test. One was the 265-cubic-incher of 205 hp; the other was a non-power pack version (with two-barrel carburetor and milder cam, etc.) which is rated at 170 hp. It is only where performance results are reported that each car is identified, since the two cars were nearly identical and equipped with PowerGlide automatic transmission, manual steering and brakes; the only major accessories were a radio and heater.

It may be mentioned here that the Chevrolet has two interesting characteristics, in addition to others described in this report: its general seating position for the driver more closely approximates that of sports car machinery than any competitive passenger car make out of Detroit. The steering wheel is nearer to the vertical and, with the seat pushed forward, almost sits in your lap. Furthermore, the variable-position seat—the back of which also approaches the vertical as the unit is tracked forward—and gives a feeling of sitting high with a commanding view of the road.

Also deserving of comment is the speedometer action, which is decidedly abnormal. Those of other makes are invariably optimistic, whereas the Chevrolet has one of the few which read slower than actual speeds. For instance, at an indicated 45, the electric fifth wheel registered 47.5 mph. At an indicated 60, actual mph was 62.5 and at 70 the car really was moving along at 71.4.

Road Test-

1956 CHEVROLET Bel-Air

Photographed by Joseph Farkas

ACCELERATION of the 205-hp is sensational, makes it honestly hotter than even larger-engined standard passenger jobs. Times for 0-to-60 mph runs ranged from 8.4 to 9.4 seconds—the variation resulting from a still-stiff transmission (stick with overdrive) in the new car. Average 0-to-30 mph was 3.2: quickest 50-to-80 mph was 9.2; standing quarter-mile, 16.4. The car's 110-mph speedometer is barely adequate for its speed clocked at 108.7 mph. Figures for the 170-hp Powerglide test car naturally were slower: 0-to-30 in 4.1 seconds: 0-to-60 mph, 11.9; 50-to-80 mph, 15.1 and top speed measured at 98.2 mph.

GAS MILEAGE check was made on the 170-hp four-door Bel Air. At steady and level speeds, it yielded 20 mpg at 30 mph, 18.9 mpg at 45 and 16 at 60. On the 205-hp two-door version, an overall tank mileage (including throttle-punching tests of 13.5 mpg. Chevrolet owners should note that it's nice to show what your car can do, but you obviously pay for such demonstrations at the gas pump. A new feature on the 1956 models is the gas tank filler neck located behind the left rear taillight, which puts it in the Cadillac and Continental class. Access is by turning a small vertical bar above light counter-clockwise to get at the gas cap.

TOP ROADABILITY and handling characteristics are qualities the Chevrolet has carried over from 1955 to 1956. Stock car racing drivers agreed that it was more than just performance that won so many races for this car in 1955; they reported that it was stable, cornered well. Since no major chassis or suspension changes were made for 1956—why fight it when you've got it made?—the same can be said for the new models. You can push this car on almost any road surface and not get into difficulty unless you're trying hard. The necessary compromise between soft, comfortable ride and a suspension firm enough to get you thru corners has been accomplished ad-

mirably. Sure, there's some body lean, but it isn't bad and, even on muddy, gravel corners, you seldom get the feeling of the car controlling you instead of vice versa. Some of the preciseness of control is lost in the higher speed ranges, particularly in a medium to strong cross-wind. The relatively light engine and spherical-joint front suspension are big factors in Chevrolet's fine roadability. (This combination, incidentally, makes it hard to believe that anyone would need power steering unless they spend most of their time parking!) The car reacts noticeably to rugged bumps, but feels very solid over the worst. Actually, only chronic complainers will find anything wrong with riding comfort.

PARKING MANEUVERABILITY is a Chevrolet long suit. It's shorter than its two major competitors, has a lighter engine. Although the steering ratio may seem higher than necessary on the highway, it helps take the curse out of squeezing into tight parking spaces. Power steering would seem to be superfluous, except maybe for the ladies. Excellent visibility, four visible fenders are definite aids in tight spots.

Styling for 1956 has moderate changes. New rear fenders (left) show family relationship with Buick, including taillight treatment. Profile of grille shows "veed" design,

helps emphasize the Cadillac-inspired flat headlight hoods. Wheel covers (right) once could have been sold as custom items a few years ago. Cutouts resemble Olds.

TECHNICAL REPORT on the 1956 Chevrolet

The 1956 Chevrolet engine comes in three sizes, as measured by horsepower output, and the chief difference, besides power kit installations, is derived from a special cam assigned to Powerglides to put them on a par with sticks.

CHEVROLET ADS are right insofar as the Powerglide equipped models go. As far as the standard model with the three-speed transmission is concerned, it still pumps 162 horses at 4400 rpm. The Powerglide, even sans power kit, kicks out 170 hp at the same engine speed. Ordered with the power kit, though, both PG and stick-shift models pump a healthy 205 hp at 4600 rpm. So, if by the "hot one" the copy writers mean the power kit machines, they're very much justified in their huffing and puffing.

THE "NEW" ENGINE

At first blush the above figures would not seem to ring quite true. PG without power kit turns out 170 hp or eight more than the similarly equipped standard-shift model yet both put out 205 when given the factory hop-up. This is the sort of thing that generates indignant mail. However, there's an explanation that will give the answer easily.

The fact of the matter is that the Chevrolet folks have slipped in a gimmick to even things up between the stick-shift and the automatic, even to the point of giving the Powerglide a slight edge if handled right. The trick is a cam with characteristics that would spell full race in large letters if seen a couple of years ago. Duration of this frightening valve tickler is a healthy 270 degrees as against 252 degrees for the cam in the regular run of the mine standard shift model. Valve lift is also higher by .0396 of an inch in the PG-equipped engine. Even

though a fairly long ramp cuts down valve acceleration and takes some of the pepper out of the cam, these characteristics make it a very hot stick indeed, ramp or no ramp. Apparently this cam is also used in the power kit engines of both standard shift and automatic equipped cars. This, with the optional 9.25-to-1 heads, four-barrel carburetor and dual exhausts explains the very hefty 205 horses gained from 265 cubic inches.

In all other respects the engine is virtually the same as the 1955 models. The block is a 90-degree Vee with a bore of 3.75 of an inch and a stroke of just three inches which still leaves it the shortest stroked engine in the industry, not counting foreign machinery. This, of course, spells long life and also a very high wind-up, a point which is readily seen in the high (for Detroit) peak speed of the power-kit rig. The high twist of 4600 rpm is not the end of it either since many of these power kit equipped jobs have been buzzed over 7000 using only the factory equipment. It may well be, however, that the rpm limit will be held down due to the fact that all the 1956 engines are equipped with hydraulic valve lifters. This is opposed to the 1955 practice in which the standard shift models were set up with solid tappets. This led to a very discouraging series of rocker stud replacements due to exuberant over-revving. The Powerglide models had the hydraulic lifters and, even in power kit form, were not subject to such failures. It wasn't that the PG owners were less enthusiastic but merely that the upper rev limit imposed by the pump-up speed of the lifters was around 6800 rpm. At speeds allowed by the solid tappets the rocker studs popped out like champagne corks at a Polish wedding.

The Chevrolet engine is the smallest and lightest V-8 in the business, a point which is rapidly making it prim transplant material. Dry weight of the engine is 469 lbs. complete with power kit; width is a mere 31 inches and length is 22 inches or three inches shorter than that other studdy, the Dodge. Height at 31 inches is the only dimension not appreciably different from the rest of the V-8 tribe.

People are continually asking why the Chevy is so cockeyed hot—why it should prune such heat waves as Buick Centurys, Mercurys and Oldsmobiles with such apparent ease. It's a good question and a

(*Continued on page* 51)

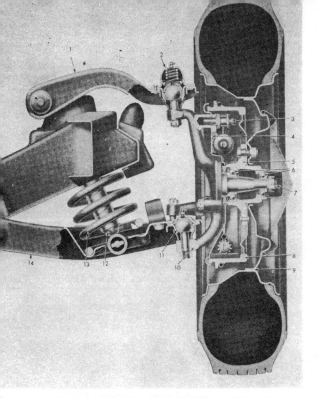

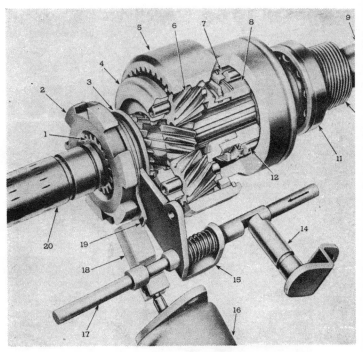

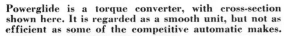

Ball-joints eliminated the kingpin in 1955, but Chevy has two additional differences from conventional cars: (1) the coil springs are set at an angle; (2) it uses no anti-roll or sway bar.

Powerglide is a torque converter, with cross-section shown here. It is regarded as a smooth unit, but not as efficient as some of the competitive automatic makes.

Chevrolet waited a long time for its overdrive and what it got was essentially a two-speed planetary box attached to rear of a three-speed transmission. Cut-in is at 26-30 mph.

Differential is all in one case which has two advantages: easier servicing or quicker gear changes in competition. Chevrolet dropped long-used closed torque tube last year.

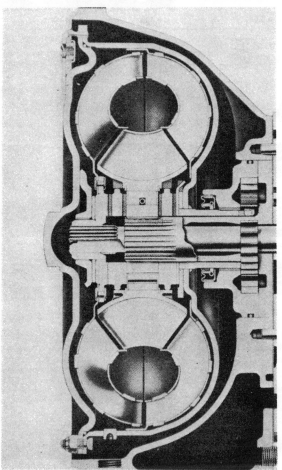

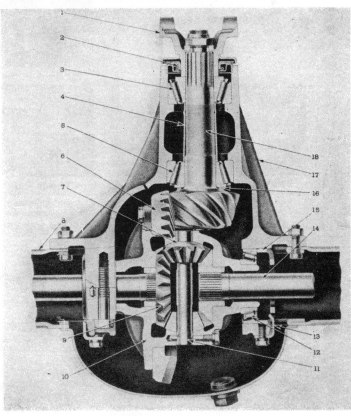

CHEVROLET'S LINE OF 1956 CARS

IF YOU plan to buy a new Chevrolet, your choice of body types is shown below. The prices indicated are those recommended by the factory and include federal taxes and normal delivery charges; they do not include options, local taxes or transportation. Other price information can be found in "Comparing the 1956 Cars" in this issue. However, the figures are a good index of the relative value of each different style and are helpful in forming a preliminary estimate—after that it's up to you and the dealer to come to terms.

ONE-FIFTY SERIES

• Business Coupe—$1799

• Two-door Sedan—$1891

• Four-door Sedan—$1934

TWO-TEN SERIES

• Four-door Sedan—$2020

• Two-door Sedan—$1977

• Four-door Hardtop—$2182

• Two-door Hardtop—$2128

• Club Coupe—$2036

BEL-AIR SERIES

• Four-door Sedan—$2133

• Two-door Sedan—$2090

• Four-door Hardtop—$2295

• Two-door Hardtop—$2241

• Convertible—$2409

STATION WAGONS

• One-Fifty Two-door—$2236

• Two-Ten Two-door—$2280

• Two-Ten Four-door 2 seats—$2328
3 seats—$2413

• Bel Air Four-door 3 seats—$2547

• Nomad Two-door—$2573

COMPARATIVE ROAD TESTS:

CHEVROLET, FORD and PLYMOUTH

This trio will probably lead in car sales for '56. Which is the one for you?

Chevrolet V-8 with "power pack" leads the horsepower parade in its class with 205 hp. But power packs are tough to get at this point.

THROUGH the years, the Chevrolet, Ford and Plymouth have become known as the "low-priced" three and have, for the most part, been the largest-selling automobiles in the United States. For a time Buick managed to displace Plymouth for third spot, but since that car is in an entirely different price range we will not consider it here. The point is, given $2,500 or less to spend, more people have been purchasing a Chevy, a Ford or a Plymouth, and competition among these three makes has gotten keener with each succeeding year. In the past three years, Chevrolet's top position has been strongly challenged by Ford, and Plymouth made a vivid comeback in 1955.

Now the 1956 models are out and thousands of people are being faced with the problem of which one to buy. We cannot really hope to make a final choice for anyone because so much that can be considered good or bad in any car is a matter of taste, but we still have definite comparisons and suggestions to make. Why not look the cars over with us and see how the three rivals measure up?

GENERAL STYLING

This is the toughest category to deal with in a critical way because it deals almost exclusively with personal taste. Actually the cars are not so very different from one another as your first impression leads you to believe. They are all striving for the same basic effect, that being to look as large as possible without being clumsy. Last year Chevrolet did come out with a rather unique and foreign-looking front grille treatment but as the months went by, GM stylists became less and less convinced that this unique approach was a wise one. Accordingly they have expanded the grille to the outer extremities of the fenders in their 1956 product giving the whole front end of the car a more massive—and more normal—look. The result is a Veed, "open-mouthed" grille effect, with parking lights at the outer edges, quite similar to the 1956 Ford. Plymouth has

stuck to the "bar-type" grille treatment which does add a certain air of distinction. But headlights are hooded exactly as on the Ford and Chevy and all three cars, viewed from the side, have that forward-leaning "shark" touch. The Plymouth's greatest claim to fame, as far as we are concerned, is its "different" wrap-around windshield, with side posts that are slanted back instead of forward so that they do not interfere with the general flowing lines of the car. Chrysler Corp. has made much of the raised "flight-sweep" rear fenders, but we feel that these do little for the appearance of the car. If bulk is what you're after, you may like the impression they give, but we found them useful only as parking guides. Still they do not really distract from the car's lines. Ford for 1956 has strengthened the Thunderbird look in its passenger-car line with bold sweeps of chrome and vivid but tasteful color schemes. We tend to give it the nod in over-all styling because of its tendency toward an uncluttered look

THE INSIDE STORY

Now let's step into the cars and see how they rate for all-around comfort, visibility, etc. The Chevrolet has the most advantageous driving position, affording the greatest visibility out the front, even for a relatively short driver. Even the top of the steering wheel is not in the line of vision of the average woman. Chevy floor pedals have a comfortable feel, too, with gas and brake almost on the same level so that both can be reached with the heel pivoting on the floor.

Ford features suspended gas and brake pedals that work smoothly but are perhaps a bit too far off the floor. Seating position and steering-wheel angle are quite comfortable for the driver, but forward visibility is not so good as with the Chevy, no doubt because the seat of the Ford is lower. The dash panel is quite handsome and the instruments easily read. The glove compartment is of a useful size.

Plymouth visibility is about on a par with Ford out the front, but not as good as Chevrolet. Out the rear, however, those high fender fins make this the easiest of the three cars to park because you can always see exactly what you are doing, no matter how short you are. This applies only if you turn around to look directly out the rear window. None of the cars has a rear-view mirror big enough to make complete use of the rear-window glass area.

As for foot pedals, the Plymouth has what is probably the best set-up of all for anyone who has gotten into the habit of using the left foot for braking in automatic-transmission cars. Here the brake pedal has an extension on the left side so that brake and gas may be applied at the same time and with equal pressure without altering the driving position.

Headroom and leg-and-hip room is about equal on

Of the three cars, Plymouth has had the biggest styling change, rear fenders having been raised considerably to give "flight sweep" look.

Ford's steering is rather a compromise between that of Plymouth and Chevy, having more feel than the former and less turns than latter system.

the three cars, both in front and in the rear. Side visibility in the rear seat is also just about the same in each case, but ventilation is possibly just a bit better in the Plymouth, the only one of the three to have a rear quarter window that actually opens. The Chevrolet rear seat is curved near the bottom at the outer edges, affording good support for the passengers sitting beside either window. This, as a matter of fact, is a safety feature.

Taking the cars apart, feature by feature, could be an endless procedure. Each one has little details that will be considered good by some people and not so good by others. All we can do is to make our own choice on the basis of one or more major factors which we consider to be most important. In view of this, our pick is the Chevrolet, because of its superior driving position and forward visibility.

HOW THEY HANDLE

At last we take each car for a ride. Immediately impressive in the Plymouth is the way it soaks up all manner of bumps and holes in the road. The only way to describe the ride of this car is "luxurious," and yet the suspension is not so soft that the Plymouth wallows or leans to an alarming degree. Fairly high speeds can be

maintained over bad roads without any side-slipping and there is never any backlash at all from the steering. This last feature is not going to be considered "good" by every driver because a certain amount of vibration in the steering serves to impart more "feel" and a certain measure of confidence. But if the Plymouth steering has less feel than Ford and Chevrolet, it is also the fastest of the three, and eliminates a lot of work on tight corners.

Speaking of corners, the Plymouth shows a nice degree of understeer, thus allowing it to break loose from the front wheels first. This is a good safety factor because it allows the driver to sort his car out in a corner that he has taken a bit too fast. The relatively soft springing does allow the Plymouth to drift possibly a little sooner than we would like on "fast" corners. This car does not track as well as either the Ford or the Chevrolet.

As for the Plymouth's push-button transmission controls, you will either love them or wish you had a lever on the steering column. For "rocking" in snow or ice it is unbeatable, but there are certain disadvantages. The buttons must be pushed rather far before they will cancel out one driving range and engage another; there is a certain danger of depressing a button half-way and failing to make a gear-change. This might be embar-

Chevrolet rated tops in forward visibility, even for a relatively short driver. Wheel rim was not in the way.

Biggest advantage of Plymouth was its abiilty to maneuver in close; steering and push-buttons both helped here.

Directional stability of the Ford is extremely good; even in a high cross wind practically no steering-wheel correction was necessary.

rassing if you parked the Plymouth in front of a store for a moment, only to have it "drive" away while you were inside. Another interesting situation might develop if you made a hurried "down-shift" from drive to low range for a steep hill or a sharp curve only to find that you are in neutral just when you need traction or engine braking. But to be honest let us admit that not one driver in a thousand will ever want to shift gears while he is moving.

Moving to the Chevrolet, we find that the ride is somewhat firmer than that on the Plymouth, but still very definitely with a big-car feel. Lean in corners is about the same but the Chevy oversteer. This means that it tends to break away from the rear wheels first and this can become pretty tricky in tight corners unless you know how to handle it, or unless you experiment with tire pressures. One good factor is that even though the steering is rather slow, it keeps you well informed as to what the wheels are doing, and you can compensate for the oversteer before it gets troublesome. Out on the open road, fast bends can be taken with precision since the car tracks well, and stability is good in cross winds. Comparing the general handling and roadability of the Plymouth and Chevrolet, we favor the Plymouth on bad roads and on tight corners and the Chevy on fast bends and "at speeds" on the open road.

The Chevrolet Powerglide is quite smooth and operates via an easily-reached lever on the steering column. Driving positions are Park, Neutral, Drive, Low and Reverse, in that order, so it is easy to go from drive to low and from reverse to low with a flick of the finger, even without taking one's eyes off the road.

Getting to the Ford, we find a number of compromises (not with quality but between the Plymouth and the Chevrolet). The ride is about as firm as on the Chevrolet, but the steering is neither "over" nor "under" but sort of neutral. In any sort of corner the Ford tracks quite well, but taken through faster, it can be "played with"—that is, slid around sideways—using both steering and gas. Balance is no better than with either of its two rivals, so this neutral steering is all a matter of steering geometry.

Ford's power steering is half-way between Plymouth and Chevrolet—both in feel and in quickness of response. It steers slower than the Plymouth and faster than the Chevy, and has more feel than the Plymouth and less than the Chevrolet. We call it a happy medium. An over-all choice among the three cars would be tough here because it depends so much on the type of driving you do. We still prefer the Plymouth for "in-close" work, but find the Ford and the Chevrolet running neck and neck in all other respects.

Brakes on all three cars were improved from last

Taken into a corner hard, the Chevrolet showed a tendency to oversteer but lean was not excessive and the car never got out of hand.

Same sort of corner taken at same speed with the Plymouth produced same amount of lean. Car understeered, slid from front wheels first.

year and actually quite good under all normal operating conditions. They can be made to fade after five or six hard applications from 60 mph, but all recover quickly and are ordinarily free from squealing and grabbing.

PERFORMANCE TESTS

The figures gotten here will surprise you, not for any other reason than that they are so close. The cars tested are the largest V-8s in each line, and here there is a preliminary story to tell. The Ford Fairlane series cars come equipped with 202-hp engines. This is without the need for an additional "power kit," and the Fairlane cars are readily available. Plymouth lists top horsepower for the V-8 without a power kit as 187, but 200-hp power-kit-fitted cars can be purchased just as

After a discussion of performance and top speed, it is only fitting that we should consider the safety angle of each of our test cars. We used to feel somewhat sneaky whenever we got onto this subject and its relation to new cars, but not any more. Detroit has been pushing safety themselves so much this year that it is almost impossible to ignore.

The Chevrolet is the unique car in this group, for a number of reasons. First of all, GM has made less of a fuss in their advertising than have Ford and Chrysler Corporation. But this does not mean that the Chevy does not have safety features to meet the competition. On the contrary, they have had dished steering wheels and safety door locks since last year!

The Chevrolet for '56 has available, as optional

Ford steering was "neutral" and car could be slid around corners. Ride was firmer than on Plymouth, about the same as the Chevrolet.

Control over bad, dirt roads was very good with Chevrolet, little front-end bobbing being experienced. Plymouth gave a softer ride.

easily. Chevrolet's top "normal" horsepower is 170; this can be raised to 205—top in the class—with their power kit.

But there is a hitch. The Chevy power kit is very difficult to get. (So difficult, in fact, that we could not get one for our test; we will report on a Chevy so equipped later in the year.) The result is this: Most popular "big" V-8 models of the Ford, Plymouth and Chevrolet have, respectively, 202, 200 and 170 hp. This may seem unfair to the Chevy, but the figures are much closer than you might think.

To 30 mph the Chevy requires 4.6 seconds, the Ford 4.7 and the Plymouth 4.5. Rear-axle ratios help Plymouth and Chevy here. Times to 50 mph are 8.8 for the Chevrolet, 8.6 for the Ford and 8.3 for the Plymouth. Note that the somewhat-lighter Plymouth still has an advantage. The same is true for the zero-to-60 mph times where the Chevy clocks 11.8 seconds, the Ford 11.9 and the Plymouth 11.6 seconds. That new Plymouth V-8 mill is a whiz.

Figures on all three of these cars could be made better if jump acceleration from a stoplight was all that was desired. But they all still have lots of punch on the "high" end, accelerating well right up over the 80-mph mark. Top speed runs are difficult to compare in view of the different conditions encountered during the tests, but here they are: the Chevrolet will do at least 105 mph, the Ford 103 and the Plymouth 104 or 105. We say "at least" because we feel that none of the timed speed runs were made under ideal conditions. But what difference does it make, anyway? Top speed will vary even with two "identical" models of the same make car. Tuning makes a lot of difference.

equipment, not only safety belts but shoulder harness. In addition, a padded dash panel can be installed.

Ford has gone all-out for safety. Their cars can be equipped, if you wish, with safety belts, padded dash panels and even padded sun visors. The dished steering wheels and safety door locks are, of course, standard equipment.

Plymouth has not been left behind. They, too, have safety wheels and doors and dashboards. But we found their seat belt installations to be most interesting. Most safety belts are slipped through the seat and bolted directly to the floor—or to the frame through a hole in the floor. But Plymouth belts are fastened to the seats and then the seats are in turn fastened by cable to the floor. This seems to us to be a very good idea because many bad accidents rip a car's seats right from their moorings, and this can be dangerous even to a driver or passenger who is "bolted" to the floor. In the Plymouth, passengers *and* seats will stay put in a crash. Or at any rate they should; we didn't perform any tests to find out.

It is difficult to rate any one car as being better or worse from the safety standpoint. The truth is you can get almost any safety feature you want on any car if you want to pay for it. The question is, "how much is your life worth to you?"

THE SUMMING UP . . .

As stated before, we cannot hope to make a final choice as to which of these three cars is the best. All should give years of faithful and pleasant service and gas mileage in each case runs to better than 20 miles

Plymouth's strong point in the handling department is on "slow" corners where fast steering eliminates "unwinding."

Chevrolet is better on "fast" corners where the stiffer springing, steering feel can be employed to good effect.

Ford showed an over-all cornering ability about half-way between Plymouth and Chevy. Traction was good in the wet.

per gallon in general long-distance travel. We refuse to give figures for any constant speed because it is impossible to drive that way on the highway, and our tests are aimed at an average for the general consumer, normal driving procedure being kept in mind at all times. Suggested basic prices, F.O.B. Detroit, are $1,952 for the Chevrolet four-door BelAire sedan, $1,964 for the four-door Ford Fairlane sedan and $1,992 for the four-door Plymouth Belvedere. You pay your money and you takes your choice. ●

COMPARING THEM AT A GLANCE...

CHEVROLET SPECIFICATIONS

ENGINE: V-8, overhead valves; bore, 3.25 in.; stroke, 3.00 in.; total displacement, 265 cu. in.; developed hp, 170 at 4,000 rpm (power kit available to raise hp to 205 at 4,600 rpm); torque, 257 lb./ft. at 2,400 rpm; compression ratio, 8 to 1; single two-barrel down-draft carburetor; mechanical fuel pump; crankcase capacity, 4 qts.; radiator capacity, 17 qts.; ignition, 12 volts.
TRANSMISSION: Powerglide torque converter.
REAR AXLE RATIO: 3.55 to 1 (Powerglide) 3.70 and 4.11 also available.
SUSPENSION: front by individual coils and hydraulic shock absorbers; rear by semi-elliptic leaf springs and hydraulic shock absorbers.
BRAKES: four-wheel hydraulic; power booster available.
DIMENSIONS: wheelbase, 115 in.; front tread, 58 in.; rear tread, 58.8 in.; width, 74 in.; height, 62 in.; over-all length, 195.6 in.; turning circle, 41.50 ft.; ground clearance, 6.5 in.; approximate dry weight, 3,200 lbs.; tires, 6.70 x 15 tubeless.

PERFORMANCE

ACCELERATION: Zero to 30 mph: 4.6 seconds.
Zero to 50 mph: 8.8 seconds.
Zero to 60 mph: 11.8 seconds.
TOP SPEED: 105 mph+.

FORD SPECIFICATIONS

ENGINE: V-8, overhead valves; bore, 3.75 in.; stroke, 3.30 in.; total displacement, 292 cu. in.; developed hp, 202 at 4,600 rpm; torque, 285 lb./ft. at 2,600 rpm; compression ratio, 8.4 to 1; single four-barrel carburetor; mechanical fuel pump; crankcase capacity, 5 qts.; radiator capacity, 20 qts.; ignition, 12 volts.
TRANSMISSION: Fordomatic torque converter with three-speed planetary gear box.
REAR AXLE RATIO: 3.22 to 1 (Fordomatic) 3.78 and 3.89 also available.
SUSPENSION: front by independent ball joint and hydraulic shock absorbers; rear by semi-elliptic leaf springs and hydraulic shock absorbers.
BRAKES: four-wheel hydraulic, 11 in.-diameter drums, power booster available.
DIMENSIONS: wheelbase, 115 in.; front tread, 58 in.; rear tread, 56 in.; width, 75.9 in.; height, 60.2 in.; over-all length, 198.5 in.; turning circle, 41 ft.; ground clearance, not available; dry weight, 3,290 lbs.; tires, 6.70 x 15 tubeless.

PERFORMANCE

ACCELERATION: Zero to 30 mph: 4.7 seconds.
Zero to 50 mph: 8.6 seconds.
Zero to 60 mph: 11:.9 seconds.
TOP SPEED: 103 mph.

PLYMOUTH SPECIFICATIONS

ENGINE: V-8, overhead valves, power pack; bore, 3.75 in.; stroke, 3.13 in.; total displacement, 277 cu. in.; developed hp, 200 at 4,400 rpm; torque, 272 lb./ft. at 2,400 rpm; compression ratio, 8 to 1; single four-barrel carburetor; mechanical fuel pump; crankcase capacity, 6 qts.; radiator capacity, 14 qts.; ignition, 12 volts.
TRANSMISSION: PowerFlite torque converter.
REAR AXLE RATIO: 3.54 to 1 (PowerFlite) 3.73 and 4.1 also available.
SUSPENSION: front by individual coil springs and wishbones with hydraulic shock absorbers; rear by semi-elliptic leaf springs; hydraulic shock absorbers.
BRAKES: four-wheel hydraulic, dual cylinder front; independent hand brake; power booster available.
DIMENSIONS: wheelbase, 115 in.; front tread 58.4 in.; rear tread, 58.5 in.; width, 75 in.; height, 60 in.; over-all length, 205 in.; turning circle, 41.- ft.; ground clearance, 5.6 in.; dry weight, 3,145 lbs.; tires 6.70 x 15 tubeless.

PERFORMANCE

ACCELERATION: Zero to 30 mph: 4.5 seconds.
Zero to 50 mph: 8.3 seconds.
Zero to 60 mph: 11.6 seconds.
TOP SPEED: 105 mph.

CHEVROLET TECHNICAL REPORT

(Continued from page 42)

hard, or rather almost impossible, one to answer.

Internally the engine is very similar to other V-8 plants and even, theoretically, inferior to some of those it shuts down readily. Like most other GM engines it is of a fairly conservative design. There are no fancy combustion chambers or valve layouts. The combustion chamber is of the wedge-type used with but two exceptions (if you count Chrysler as one line) throughout the industry. Valves are in-line and slightly canted but not drastically so. Pistons are flat-topped slipper type items with provision for controlled expansion. Material is aluminum alloy, tin plated and only three rings are used. Wrist pins are pressed into the rod and offset in the piston toward the major thrust side. The connecting rods are of drop forged steel and, due to the very short stroke involved, are exceedingly short, stout and stiff. Rod bearings are .817 inches long by 1.9995 inches in diameter, giving a monstrous amount of bearing area and partially explaining the engine's ability to wind up without coming unglued. The crankshaft is also of forged steel and runs in five massive main bearings, further explaining the engine's sticking ability.

The cam and valve system comes the closest to giving a clue to the Chevrolet's dusting powers. The standard cam is timed as follows: Intake opens 18 degrees before top center and closes 54 degrees after bottom center; the exhaust opens 52 degrees before bottom center and closes 20 degrees after top center for a total duration of 252 degrees on both intake and exhaust. The Powerglide and power kit cam is, as was said earlier, a goodish bit hotter: Intake opens 26°30′ before top center and closes 63°30′ after bottom center; the exhaust opens 66°30′ before bottom center and closes 23°30′ after top center. This latter item is a power cam pure and simple yet it has sufficient timing and lift at the valve (.5598 of an inch) to give plenty of high speed suds. The hydraulic lifters undoubtedly soak up a few of these beans but by no means all. In point of size the valves in the Chevrolet are actually smaller than those in the engines of the other cars in the same price and size category and lift is only a slight shade higher. Apparently it is the timing that counts in this case, both cams being just a shade hotter than those of the competitors. With this partial attempt at explaining the Chev's "heat" we'll beg the question and, emulating the factory, duck around the corner when it's asked in the future. One thing's sure—the combination works as many a red-faced big-car owner will reluctantly attest.

Three transmission options are offered: standard or conventional, overdrive and, of course, Powerglide.

The conventional gearing is anything but close range, a point on which it fails to compare with its strongest rival in the low-priced field. You can have any set of ratios you want as long as you want direct in high, 1.68 in second and 2.94 in low. This sort of spacing seems strange in light of the output of the Chevrolet engine and in view of the neatly spaced ratios of the competing makes. However, the fantastic engine speeds available with the Chev might serve to make up for it. The same ratios are used with the overdrive which has a ratio of 0.7 or a kick-up of 0.3 over direct. Minimum cut-in speed of the overdrive unit is between 26 and 30 mph.

Chevrolet's automatic is the well-known Powerglide unit which is of the torque converter type with planetary gears. There is only one kickdown gear which is very low indeed at 1.82-to-1. This transmission depends primarily on the torque converter for multiplication and automatic kickdown is provided only up to 50 mph, a factor which can become a real nuisance in mountain driving. The unit can be force shifted but only the two speeds of low and high are available which gives that other make a distinct advantage. In fact, it's only too bad that Chevrolet's transmissions can't keep up with their new engines. The Chev gearbox has always been one of those items which led to the term "stove-bolt" in years gone by. The $83 Cragar gear treatment is about the only answer unless one can talk a friendly dealer into ordering the 1956 Corvette conventional transmission gears which seem to have a better split all along the way.

In the drive-shaft department Chevrolet has gone the way of the rest of the industry in using an exposed, open-tube shaft, discarding the torque tube layout used in years gone by. This tube is a fairly hefty item 58.5 inches long, made up of three-inch by .065-wall tubing. Yoke and spider or trunnion type universals are used at either end.

The rear end is a fairly standard semifloating hypoid unit with the pinion, ring gear and attendant bearings all in one removable case. This makes things easy to change gears, a definite factor for competition purposes since gear changes can be accomplished merely by swapping cases. For the average citizen it means less service time since everything can come out in one hunk, a point not to be overlooked in these days of time-and-material repair charges. Ratios available are 4.11-to-1 for overdrive equipped cars, 3.70-to-1 for standard transmissions and 3.55-to-1 for Powerglide machinery. Due to the unit case, these can be swapped around at will.

From the point of view of servicing and accessibility to the underside of the car the Chevrolet frame is an excellent piece of work. From the point of view of rigidity, however, the standard frame leaves somewhat to be desired. It has two crossmembers, one at the front and one at the rear. Convertibles, the Corvette and some wagon models have a sturdy X-brace in the center. Side rails are strong box members with a good cross-sectional area which may make up to some extent for the lack of internal bracing.

Springing is by coils on the front and longitudinal semi-elliptic leaves on the rear. The front springs are unique in that they are set at an angle with the upper ends canted inward rather than set vertically as in other cars. Suspension arms are of the S.L.A. (short and long arm) type and no kingpins are used, Chevrolet having gone to ball-joints in 1955 with the new spring layout. Tube shock absorbers are mounted inside the spring helix and no anti-roll or sway bar is used, the manufacturer insisting that none is needed or desired—a point with which one is free to agree or to disagree depending on where one wants one's roll center. There is one point here, though, Chevrolet handling is, for Detroit machinery, of the best (though still not perfect).

Although Chevrolet has 11-inch diameter brakes the width of the drums is smaller than most, giving a total of 158 square inches of braking surface. Effectiveness, however, is quite high. Shoe width is two inches on the front and 1.75 inches on the rear which follows normal practice except that width is smaller by .25-inch on the front than is the case with several competitors. Wheel cylinder bores on the rear brakes are also smaller than average. Despite these theoretical faults, however, Chevrolet's braking is generally good and little if any fade is experienced except under the most severe conditions.

Steering, as in all GM cars, is on the slow side at 25-to-1 with mechanical control and 23-to-1 with the power unit. The mechanical unit is a semi-reversible recirculating ball type set-up and is extremely smooth. The power steering is a Saginaw unit set up to assist rather than to take over the job of handling. Assistance is zero up to three pounds pull on the wheel rim. As pressure is increased on the rim, power is applied in proportion to the force necessary to turn the front wheels. The final effort is up to 80 per cent of that required. Hydraulic pressure is supplied by a pump mounted on the rear of a special precision generator. Pressure supplied is 750 psi.

All in all, little more need be said other than that the Chevrolet has proven itself a winner in 1955. For 1956, as the man said: "The hot one's even hotter." •

Road Test:
THE 205 HP CHEVROLET
"the hot one is even hotter"

LAST YEAR we tested a Chevrolet V-8 equipped with power-pack and overdrive, the only test of a car so equipped which was published. At the time (Feb. 1955) we said "it certainly appears that a Chevrolet V-8 with optional 180 bhp engine and 4.11 axle will out-accelerate any American car on the market today!"

Due to the tremendous interest which last year's test aroused we arranged with the Harry Mann Chevrolet Co., Los Angeles (the largest Corvette dealer in the USA!), for a test of a 1956 Chevrolet equipped to our specifications. The new power-pack gives 205 bhp, up 14%, and due to our previous experience with overdrive (the 1955 car turned a higher top speed in direct drive than in overdrive) we specified a car without overdrive. Also, the radio and heater were omitted to save weight, but even so the new car checked out only 10 pounds under last year's model 210 sedan-coupe.

The startling 111 mph top speed (3 timed runs *each* gave 111.1 mph) of this automobile furnishes a perfect opportunity for an object lesson on axle ratios.

axle ratio	4.11	3.70	3.55	2.88(od)
rpm at				
111 mph	5700	5140	4940	3990

Since the engine develops it peak bhp at 4600 rpm, it is possible that the car might go still faster with the 3.55 axle which is standard equipment on the powerglide models. However, the 3.70 ratio is an excellent compromise as can be seen by comparing last year's acceleration times with those obtained on the 1956 test car.

	180 bhp 4.11 axle	205 bhp 3.70 axle	time gain
0-30 mph	2.9	3.0	——
0-40 mph	5.7	4.1	1.6
0-50 mph	7.2	6.8	0.4
0-60 mph	9.7	9.0	0.7
0-70 mph	13.1	11.1	2.0
0-80 mph.	18.8	16.5	2.3
0-90 mph	28.0	21.8	6.2
standing ¼ mi.	17.4	16.6	0.8

This table shows that the 14% increase in horsepower more than offsets the 10% reduction in axle ratio. It might also be noted that the improvement in 0-to-40 and 0-to-70 times are partially the result of higher speed shift points, for last year's test car had to shift from 1st gear at 34 to 37 mph and from 2nd at 61 to 66 mph. Incidentally the 1956 car has hydraulic valve lifters, whereas the 1955 car did not. Nevertheless, valve bounce speed remains the same at about 5600 rpm!

One unusual aspect of the acceleration curve (see data panel) is worthy of mention. The engine's torque curve must be very good in the upper rpm range, since this is the first time we have ever plotted a "curve" which gave absolutely straight lines, through the gears. Normally the acceleration curve in each gear is a mathematical function derived from the engine's torque curve. The 1956 power-pack gives only 3% more peak torque, but at 4600 rpm the torque is 234 ft-lbs as compared to only 205 ft-lbs in 1955. This is a gain of 14% and more importantly a drop of only 12.7% below the peak torque at 3000 rpm as compared to a drop of 21% in the 1955 model.

The Tapley meter pulling power readings indicate a loss of somewhat more than the 10% that might be expected from the change in axle ratio but the drag figures (coasting test) show considerably higher than last year. However, as we have explained several times before, the drag readings are not reliable to an accuracy much closer than plus or minus 10%.

Driving a large car such as this with a wheelbase only 9% shorter than a Cadillac, is not conducive to much ease of mind in heavy traffic, but the extraordinarily high seating position for the driver negates this feeling to some extent. Out on the open road the Chevrolet is very pleasant to drive for hour after hour at high speed. The ride appears to be a little firmer than some of its competitors and the re-instated front anti-roll bar definitely reduces roll on corners, as compared to the 1955 model. Like all American cars, it can be cornered at speeds which closely approach that of a vigorously driven sports car, but the operation demands dexterity, muscles and "grit" bordering on the foolhardy.

The 3-speed manual transmission is surprisingly noisy on the indirect gears and, like last year, we found the control linkage an absolute nuisance, even when making lazy shifts. It is noisy, sloppy and impossible to throw fast shifts without bending the control rods. The car starts off with a rush even in 2nd gear, but the enthusiast purchaser would be well advised to order the new Corvette "stick-shift" controls (see page 27) and have them installed on the floor. Some people claim that all companies are neglecting their "stick-shift" cars to encourage sales of the automatic transmission, which almost appears to be true, in this case.

Without a doubt the greatest charm of this car is its smooth, quiet running engine. Even though the compression ratio is extremely high (9.25 to 1) it was impossible to make it "ping" on full throttle, at any speed. Once or twice we detected a slight knock on part throttle at very low speed when lugging and on a cold (35°F) start, after sitting all night, one of the hydraulic tappets "tapped" for about 10 seconds. But, the surge of power (actually torque) is there at all times and knowing of the ultra-short stroke, one gets the impression that this engine would be impossible to "blow-up" even under the most brutal treatment.

In short, the 1956 Chevrolet is an even better performer than last year and equally important, it handles slightly better.

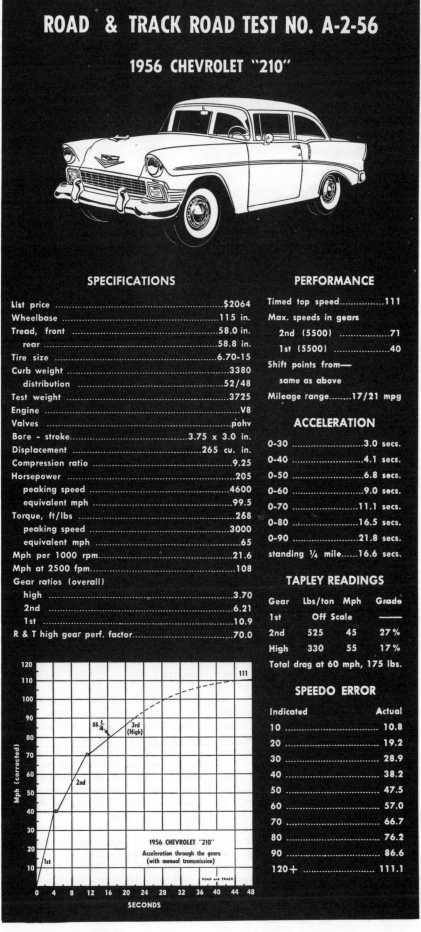

ROAD & TRACK ROAD TEST NO. A-2-56

1956 CHEVROLET "210"

SPECIFICATIONS

List price	$2064
Wheelbase	115 in.
Tread, front	58.0 in.
rear	58.8 in.
Tire size	6.70-15
Curb weight	3380
distribution	52/48
Test weight	3725
Engine	V8
Valves	pohv
Bore - stroke	3.75 x 3.0 in.
Displacement	265 cu. in.
Compression ratio	9.25
Horsepower	205
peaking speed	4600
equivalent mph	99.5
Torque, ft/lbs	268
peaking speed	3000
equivalent mph	65
Mph per 1000 rpm	21.6
Mph at 2500 fpm	108
Gear ratios (overall)	
high	3.70
2nd	6.21
1st	10.9
R & T high gear perf. factor	70.0

PERFORMANCE

Timed top speed	111
Max. speeds in gears	
2nd (5500)	71
1st (5500)	40
Shift points from—	
same as above	
Mileage range	17/21 mpg

ACCELERATION

0-30	3.0 secs.
0-40	4.1 secs.
0-50	6.8 secs.
0-60	9.0 secs.
0-70	11.1 secs.
0-80	16.5 secs.
0-90	21.8 secs.
standing ¼ mile	16.6 secs.

TAPLEY READINGS

Gear	Lbs/ton	Mph	Grade
1st	Off Scale		—
2nd	525	45	27%
High	330	55	17%
Total drag at 60 mph, 175 lbs.			

SPEEDO ERROR

Indicated	Actual
10	10.8
20	19.2
30	28.9
40	38.2
50	47.5
60	57.0
70	66.7
80	76.2
90	86.6
120+	111.1

1956 CHEVROLET "210"
Acceleration through the gears
(with manual transmission)

ROAD and TRACK

53

'56 CHEVROLET ROAD TEST

Some say we were too enthusiastic about the '55 Chevy. They may say so again this year. Read this test before you decide that we're biased

AN MT RESEARCH REPORT

STAYING WITH A GOOD THING, Chevrolet billboards tell us "The Hot One's Even Hotter." And they've got something to back up their insinuation that—saleswise or NASCAR-wise—'55 was a hot year indeed.

But what about the '56? You see only a small part of the Chevy changeover on those billboards or in the showrooms, for engine modifications, minor chassis changes and additional models in the line help dress up what would normally be a simple 2nd-year facelift story.

Test car: Most deluxe 2-door hardtop, equipped with Powerglide, power steering and brakes, powerpack V8, 6-passenger seatbelt installation, best radio, biggest heater available.

Other options: Accessory and convenience options include nearly anything you can think of or afford—air conditioning ($125 cheaper this year), power-moved seat and windows, unique option of seatbelts *and* shoulder harness, padded, glareproof dashboard top covering. Desirable option again this year, electric windshield wipers are worth slight ($11) extra cost, but may be installed without order in your car on delivery depending on where you live. (Chevy vacuum wipers have no booster, aren't installed on cars assembled in or sent to states like California, where this setup isn't okayed by legislature.) Turn signals are standard on all '56s, powerpack is $25 cheaper than in '55.

Power choices, available in any of Chevrolet's 19 models (including 2 new 9-passenger station wagons, 2 new 4-door hardtop sedans), range from 140-horsepower 6 (same engine in Powerglide and standard-shift cars this year) thru 162- and 170-horsepower V8s, to 205-hp powerpack engine. A pre-Daytona presstime announcement brings another power option to light: dual quad (2 4-barrel carb) manifold, true Corvette cam with mechanical lifters and lightweight valves;

cylinder heads have larger intake and exhaust passages. Corvette's center-takeoff exhaust manifold is topped with a pair of oil-wetted (not oil-bath) aircleaners. Output is 225 bhp and it can be had in *any* model, stick-shift or Powerglide.

Sturdy 6 has higher compression ratio (8 to 1), higher-lift camshaft, hydraulic lifters. (Last year's 123- and 136-hp sixes are not available for '56.) Lowest-output V8 remains unchanged, is used only with 3-speed and overdrive transmissions. The 170-hp (Powerglide only) engine had no counterpart in '55, when powerpack raised 162-hp engine to 180; it differs from basic V8 only in having a higher-lift camshaft; both have 2-barrel carburetor, single exhaust manifold. All engines, regardless of transmission used, have hydraulic valve lifters.

Scanning the option sheet you'll find that you can now have dual exhausts on station wagons (or sedan deliveries) with powerpack V8s; change in gas tank contour makes this possible for '56. Revised cylinder block casting and reshaped oil pan (for steering gear clearance) lets you order a built-in, full-flow type oil filter at extra cost (last year's oil filter was the bypass type).

Engine: Test car's high-output V8 gains 14 per cent power increase over '55 thru 2 major design changes: The same high-lift camshaft as used in the 170-hp V8 (not the '55 Corvette cam, as rumored, but a cam with less lift and better low-speed performance than the sports car's cam provides), and a compression ratio boost to 9.25 to 1 ('55 engines, other '56s have 8.0 to 1 ratio).

Internal changes include modified intake manifold heat riser (enlarged passages for greater volume of hot gases to aid vaporization of fuel, prevent carburetor icing), deeper heat grooving in throttle body of 4-barrel carburetor for improved warm-up. Looking at a '55 and '56 powerpack Chevy from beneath, you'd no-

tice a difference in exhaust pipe setups; '56 has longer mufflers and shorter exhaust pipes that are designed to minimize exhaust noise.

A mid-'55 change was made in automatic choke operation to permit quicker hot-engine restarting; other changes (exclusive to '56s) were made to water temperature gauge and sending unit for quicker, more accurate readings; sparkplugs are now the 4-rib type with deep ribs on the ceramic body to increase surface distance between plug terminal and body. This gives resistance to spark "flash-over" (bypassing the electrodes), permitting the plug to function normally even under adverse conditions.

Giving the V8 greater high-speed output thru higher compression ratio and camshaft changes necessarily raises engine rpms; this fact makes you wonder why hydraulic lifters are standard this year in most V8s, excluding only the just-announced hottest version. Chevrolet engineering sources tell us that at announcement time last fall, mechanical lifters were scheduled as an option to ward off hydraulic lifter pump-up under tough circumstances. But Chevrolet engineers pointed out that cars in family service certainly don't need them. Because of this, and the competitive advantage of having hydraulic lifters (they're quieter in operation than solid lifters) in most all engines, they had no qualms about dropping mechanical lifters for this year.

Other things new about the engine's accessories boil down to the full-flow oil filter, heavier clutch for powerpack V8s. Filter came about thru increased demand from truck owners who need the heavy-duty filter under dusty, dirty conditions; increased V8 truck orders made it practical to switch to the integral filter in all V8s. Beefed-up clutch came as a natural byproduct of higher torque and rpms. Clutch now has woven asbestos face material instead of molded type, has pressure plate of coil springs replacing former diaphragm spring, and pressure-plate ventilation is aided by a heat-dissipating, arched cover.

WHAT THE CAR IS LIKE TO DRIVE

Exit and entry: Many drivers stepping into the '56 Chevy will find that the steering wheel comes a little closer to their legs than in most cars; but the seat-to-wheel relationship doesn't hinder getting in or out of the driver's side.

Driving position: Long-legged drivers will find the steering wheel nudging their right thigh as they step on the brake pedal (particularly true of standard brake setups); test car's low-set power brake pedal alleviated much of this discomfort. The tallest of our drivers mentioned no discomfort, but felt that additional rearward seat travel would be welcome. Combination of high seat, low-set wheel spells good control, untiring long-mileage trips.

Vision: Chevrolet wraparound windshield and wiper setup rates praise on 2 major counts: glass is free of bothersome distortion, wipers work efficiently when needed to clear snow or road grime. (We disliked noise made as wiper blades hit base molding at the center under full-speed operation; trouble has been eliminated in cars built after about January 15.

Chevy's standard inside rear-view mirror is still not wide enough to take full advantage of the broad expanse of rear glass, yet to put a wider mirror in the present one's position constitutes forward-quarter blindspot. (Panel-mounted mirror was used in '53 hardtops, wasn't as satisfactory as present mirror when middle passenger blocked all view to rear.) Altho '56 hood is longer than 55's, forward vision remains excellent; front fenders are easy to see, but rear ones aren't readily in view from normal seating position.

Instrument panel: Instruments and their positions remain unchanged. Crowned panel houses high-set speedometer, fuel and temperature gauges, ammeter, oil pressure warning lights; all are directly in front of driver, all are easy to see and read.

Operation of controls: Light switch at left (includes instrument light control with full-range rheostat) and cigarette lighter at right of instrument group are handy for driver (altho passengers reach into control area to use the lighter). Ashtray at driver's side of center glove compartment is handier for driver than passengers. Legible, positive Powerglide quadrant rests at base of fan-shaped instrument housing; easy-to-use, T-handled parking brake is at left of steering column, joins with transmission parking pawl for positive rear-wheel lockup.

Chevrolet safety belts are unique among those offered this year. Loose, "outside"

COLIN CREITZ

end of belt terminates in a flat, slotted metal plate; to fasten belt, you simply poke this plate into the buckle housing on the other end of the strap—there's no loose belt to draw thru the buckle. Spring tension within the buckle snaps a "finger" into the slotted plate, gripping it until released by an upward pull on the housing (like conventional buckle setup). Simple belt-length adjustment is at the buckle end, where you run the belt thru a knurled roller within the housing. Thus, when you release the catch, the loose-end plate is freed immediately—again, there's no surplus length of belt to run thru the catch. (Dealers are finding many belt-buyers among new-car and old-car owners, according to local agencies which we canvassed in vain looking for Chevy's optional shoulder harness installed in a '56.)

Ease of handling: Owners of '55 Chevys will possibly notice slightly truer steering, maybe a little more steering wheel steadiness, particularly on cars equipped with power steering. This boost to handling ease is the result of a one-degree increase in caster angle. Steering arm ends were raised slightly to retain correct steering geometry; but this change for the better is coupled with the need for adding shims to the steering knuckle stops to keep front wheels from striking the frame in a hard, tight turn; result is a 3½-inch increase in turning diameter, a change unnoticed by MT's drivers, for the car remains very easy to maneuver in tight spots.

Not only do we admire the steering ease of the standard sedan, but believe you will be surprised to find that power steering isn't as noticeable as you might think. Chevy power steering, driven via shaft from the generator, doesn't alter the number of lock-to-lock wheel turns over the standard system; standard or power steering is vast improvement over the pre-'55 Chevy set-ups because of stability of ball-joint front end.

Without the steering boost, Chevy is amazingly easy to handle at normal and high road speeds. Only in parking will power steering really be appreciated, for the front wheels of any of our cars are generally hard to turn when the car is barely in motion or not moving at all. (Some feel that power steering is more practical on the Chevy 6 than the V8, for the in-line engine adds some 30 pounds to the front end.) There was no disturbing steering wheel pull or vibration when crossing cartracks, going off road shoulders, driving in ruts.

Acceleration: MT has probably expended more complimentary copy on the V8's acceleration than on any other phase of Chevy performance; but it is an impressive machine when you realize that small-size V8's piston displacement (lowest of the Big 3 powerpack V8s) puts out surprising get-up-and-go.

Where the new cam should make its biggest showing—50-80 mph—time was lowered 3.5 seconds from stock 55's time,

photos by Jim Lodge and Al Kidd

0.9 seconds from '55 powerpack's 12.9-second time. New powerpack was noticeably livelier than last year's 182-hp job at turnpike speeds, but regardless of the fact that the '56 went faster, it *felt* no better at low speeds. Multi-carb powerpack should be better at low speeds only.

Best times in all tests were in DRIVE range only; holding Powerglide in LOW (past DRIVE's 58-mph automatic shift point) for faster times was futile.

Braking: One of the finest features introduced by Chevy in '55 continues to impress us—absence of nosedive under all stopping conditions, including panic stops. This reaction comes from resistance built into front suspension geometry, doesn't utilize control rod or bars. (Upper control arm is tilted, giving effect of radius rod as rotational force of suspension tries to counteract downward force of brake stop; utilizing forces that cause car to nosedive, Chevy suspension reduces dive by some 45 per cent.) Brakes play an important part in the control of nosedive. Stationary brake shoes resist turning drums when brakes are applied; and since brake shoes, wheel cylinder and anchor pin are all anchored to the spindle support, brakes exert a twisting force on the support in the direction of the turning wheel, setting up the force to activate dive control.

Brakes, unchanged mechanically, are good-sized (11-inch drums), bonded-lining type, with total lining area on the smallish side (2-inch front lining width, 1¾-inch lining width on rear wheels), but braking effectiveness is on the high side. In MT's fade tests, there was no sign of fade until 8th stop of the 12-stop series (repeated normal-but-hard stops from 60 mph at a fixed deceleration rate). After that, fade increased until 11th and 12th stops—the last stop under full fade condition. (But in our analysis form, we wrote "Very good for low pedal," meaning that there was some "pedal" left; as fade condition increases, so does ineffective pedal travel. In severe cases, a low-set power brake pedal which offers little mechanical leverage can be flat on the floorboard,

even tho there may be some braking ability left.) Panic-type stop immediately after completion of brake checks resulted in erratic swerve to one side, but brakes returned to normal after about 2 minutes of 50 mph driving.

Roadability: Rating a tie for tops in our evaluation of the '55 test cars, Chevy not only continues to rate praise, but is bucking for more kudos thru a couple of suspension changes.

Some of the unwanted axle movement (and resultant wheel bounce on washboard road surfaces) noted in '55 has been dampened not by struts or shock absorber changes, but by the simple expedient of widening the rear spring hangers an inch; this allows more rubber in the bushing to resist compression from axle sidethrusts. Test car's rear wheels bounced more independently than before, when whole rear end was prone to move from line of travel. Directional stability—more important in power steering setups where there's some loss of road feel to the driver—has been improved, say Chevrolet engineers, by the previously mentioned change in front-end alignment.

Not many things can upset Chevy's composure on the road; it weathers normal rigors with ease. Only when it's bounced hard by a bump, or rocked into a chuckhole in the midst of a fast turn does it betray its relatively light weight and semi-stiff suspension and skip from its initial track. But there's no reason to panic; recovery from either bumps, dips or potholes is rapid, non-jarring in most cases, and free from wallowing or pitching.

A wider spring perch greatly reduces sidesway and hopping in the rear end, giving better handling characteristics, as do the ball-joints and tilted control arm in the front end. The tilting lessens nosedive due to braking by 45 per cent. Steering linkage has been altered and turn ratios changed to give driver further ease in steering and stopping

Ride: We're often inclined to be so wrapped up in the Chevy's handling, acceleration and roadability virtues that we tend to treat ride lightly. But there's no reason to dismiss it, because it's good. Not on the soft side, Chevy ride benefits from car's inherent stability—that is, passengers aren't pitched or rocked from side to side on twisting roads, or see-sawed back and forth in stop-and-go driving.

Seats aren't soft either, but they soak up a great deal of chassis movement, level out most minor disturbances. Washboard roads are felt thruout the body, aren't too objectionable on a seat-of-the-pants evaluation. Test car's seatbelts, aside from giving feeling of security to passengers, were found to be a substantial aid against centrifugal force of hard cornering.

WHAT THE CAR IS LIKE TO LIVE WITH

Riding in the front seat: Your passengers shouldn't have any complaint. Doors open wide, stay put at stop positions. If you're used to a sedan, you'll find hardtop's roofline unblocking your hat.

Legroom is about average, regardless of seat position; headroom, tho good, was about 1½ inches less than in 55's 4-door sedan test car. (Chevy's new 4-door hardtop shares lower overall height dimension with 2-door hardtop; front seat interior dimensions of both hardtops are reduced roughly ½ to 1½ inches compared to standard sedan.)

Riding in the rear seat: Hardtop's split seat is set up for maximum ease of getting into rear seat from passenger's side; but getting into rear seat from driver's side, you'll find that left-front seatback doesn't fold forward (*Continued on page* 68)

P E R F O R M A N C E

MT ROAD TEST

'56 CHEVROLET V8
Bel Air 2-door hardtop with powerpack and Powerglide

	'56	**'55**
	(205-bhp engine)	(162-bhp engine)
ACCELERATION	From Standing Start 0-30 mph 4.2 0-60 mph 10.7 Quarter-mile 18.3 and 76 mph	From Standing Start 0-30 mph 4.3 0-60 mph 12.3 Quarter-mile 19.0 and 71 mph
	Passing Speeds 30-50 mph 3.9 50-80 mph 12.0	Passing Speeds 30-50 mph 4.4 50-80 mph 15.5
TOP SPEED	Fastest run 109.1 Slowest 106.0 Average of 4 runs 108.0	Fastest run 97.8 Slowest 96.3 Average of 4 runs 97.3
FUEL CONSUMPTION	Used Mobilgas Special Steady Speeds 20.8 mpg @ 30 19.4 mpg @ 45 16.6 mpg @ 60 13.6 mpg @ 75	Used Mobilgas Special Steady Speeds 20.6 mpg @ 30 19.2 mpg @ 45
	Stop-and-Go Driving 11.9 mpg over measured course 14.2 mpg tank average for 800 miles	Stop-and-Go Driving 13.7 mpg over measured course 14.5 mpg tank average for 1241 miles
STOPPING DISTANCE	141 feet from 60 mph	146 feet from 60 mph
BRAKE FADE	Slight on 8th stop from 60 Complete on 12th stop Complete recovery 2 minutes	
SPEEDOMETER ERROR	Read 31 at true 30, 47 at 45, 63 at 60, and 78 at 75	Read 29 at true 30, 44 at 45, 60 at 60, and 76 at 75 101 at top speed

S P E C I F I C A T I O N S

ENGINE: Ohv V8. Bore 3.75 in. Stroke 3.00 in. Stroke/bore ratio 0.80:1. Compression ratio 9.25:1. Displacement 265 cu. in. Advertised bhp 205 @ 4600 rpm. Bhp per cu. in. 0.773. Piston travel @ max. bhp 2300 ft. per min. Max. bmep 152.5 psi. Max. torque 268 lbs.-ft. @ 3000 rpm.

TRANSMISSION: Standard transmission is 3-speed synchromesh with helical gears. Automatic transmission is Powerglide, 3-element torque converter with planetary gears. Overdrive transmission is standard shift with planetary gearset.

REAR-AXLE RATIOS: Conventional 3.70, Powerglide 3.55, Overdrive 4.11.

RATIOS: Drive 1.82 x converter ratio and 1.00 x converter ratio; Low and Reverse 1.82 x converter ratio. Maximum converter ratio at stall 2.1:1.

STEERING: Turns lock to lock 5.34, mechanical and power. Overall ratio: mechanical 25.7:1, power 23.3:1. TYPE (Mechanical and

Power): semi-reversible recirculating ball.

WEIGHT: Test car weight 3760 lbs. Test car weight-bhp ratio 18.34:1.

TIRES: 6.70 x 15 tubeless.

PRICES: (Prices are for 8-cylinder models; 6-cylinder models $92 less.) ONE-FIFTY business coupe $1799, 2-door sedan $1891, 4-door sedan $1934, 2-door station wagon $2236. TWO-TEN 2-door sedan $1977, 4-door sedan $2020, club coupe $2036, 2-door hardtop $2128, 4-door hardtop $2182, 2-door station wagon $2280, 4-door station wagons $2328 and $2413. BEL AIR 2-door sedan $2090, 4-door sedan $2133, 2-door hardtop $2241, 4-door hardtop $2295, convertible $2409, 4-door station wagon $2547, Nomad station wagon $2673.

ACCESSORIES: Powerglide $179, overdrive $108, power brakes $37, power steering $92, power windows $107, 2-way power seat $103, radios $85, $64 and $105, heaters $42 and $65, air conditioning $431.

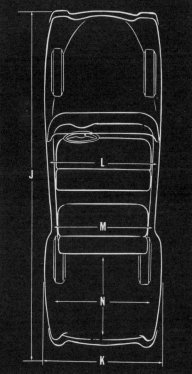

DIMENSIONS

A	FRONT OVERHANG 34.4	H	FRONT HEADROOM 35.6
B	WHEELBASE 115	I	REAR HEADROOM 35.6
C	REAR OVERHANG 48.1	J	OVERALL LENGTH 197.5
D	OVERALL HEIGHT 60.5 (62.0 unloaded)	K	OVERALL WIDTH 73.7
E	MINIMUM GROUND CLEARANCE 6.5 (at exhaust pipe)	L	FRONT SHOULDER ROOM 56.8
F	FRONT LEGROOM 43.7	M	REAR SHOULDER ROOM 56.4
G	REAR LEGROOM 42.6	N	TRUNK CAPACITY N/A

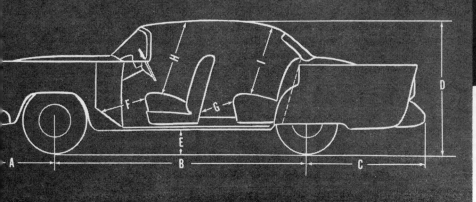

Because no one knows as much about stock cars as the men who race them, SPEED AGE has chosen a group of stock car drivers to test America's newest and most interesting cars. Every month a well known driver will put the nation's best cars through tortuous trials to bring SPEED AGE readers the inside story on performance and handling.

Jimmy Reece

TRACK TESTS THE 1956

Jimmy Reece stands before the new 1956 Chevrolet before starting his test runs for his report on the "wringing out" at the Willow Springs course.

1956 CHEVROLET 210	
0-30	4.7
0-50	8.6
0-60	11.3
Top Speed	105 mph

SPECIFICATIONS

Cylinders	V-8
Horsepower	205
Carburetor	4-barrel
Displacement	265 cu. in.

Test car courtesy of Harry Mann Chevrolet, 5735 Crenshaw Blvd., Los Angeles, California.

By JIMMY REECE

TRACK TESTING TWO OF THE leading low-price production automobiles proved quite an interesting experience to me, a professional race driver planning a strong campaign for the 1956 stock car circuit.

Over a period of one week, I tested a 1956 Chevrolet and a '56 Ford. To me, it's interesting from a competitive driving standpoint, but I can well imagine the rivalry and exciting debate that rages among average motorists who come to the races to cheer for their particular choice.

I drove the 1956 Chevrolet in an exclusive track test for SPEED AGE.

covering an extensive run over the highways as well as over the twisting road racing course at Willow Springs, Calif. The latter, in my opinion, was the greatest test of all, since the ruggedness of the S turns and those uphill and downhill runs offer a tremendous test of any car's handling characteristics.

Our car was a two-door sedan, of the "Two-Ten" series produced by Chevrolet. It was equipped with the optional "power pack" which is now available to Chevrolet buyers in the form of a Super Turbo-Fire V-8 engine. The extra goodies include a duel exhaust system, thinner head

FORD AND CHEVROLET

gaskets and four-barrel carburetion, all of which gives the power plant a boost to 205 hp.

The four-barrel carburetor has a deeper heat grooving in the throttle body, similar to the two-barrel carbs for improved warm-up characteristics. The duel exhausts include unusually long mufflers with shorter pipes to cut down on exhaust boom. Actually, it makes for a smoother, more mellow tone.

Road testing the car on the way to Willow Springs for the track test, I was impressed first of all with the quickness of the steering. I like a car with quick steering because it helps keep you out of trouble on sharp turns when you have to crank the wheel from lock to lock. On the track, especially, slow steering can keep you pretty busy in the corners. In addition to being quick, steering was easy, almost like power steering. This is due to Chevrolet's ball-race set up which cuts down much of the normal friction.

My first adverse criticism of the car came as we rolled along over the winding Ridge Route heading into the San Fernando Valley on the way to Willow Springs. The road climbs uphill and winds like a snake until reaching the summit. From there it goes downhill, still winding into tight left and right hand turns. Taking these at speed, the car cornered well but, on exceptionally hard turns, the engine cut out. This is not an uncommon factor in racing, and it is due to carburetor slushing from the sharp corners. On a race track, where turns are all left hand, this problem is eliminated by wedging one side of the carburetor.

In this particular case, however, where slushing was evident on both left and right hand turns, raising of the float level in the carburetor probably would have helped a great deal. This, of course, might mean a drop in economy, but you cannot expect economy if you are looking for power and getaway.

Before leaving for Willow Springs, I inflated all four tires to forty pounds. This was in the interest of safety while putting the car through the rugged turns at the track. Over-inflating the tires took away that soft ride over the bumps of normal highway driving, but it helps eliminate "roll over" when taking sharp turns on a race track. That is, riding on the rim of the tire due to the car leaning from punishing racing speed and handling.

At that, the ride was not extremely hard under normal conditions. In fact, it was surprisingly smooth except for the bumps of a railroad crossing and excessive bumps in the road surface. Other than that, the car rode very well and I'm used to riding on heavier, stiffer shocks anyway. My own pleasure car is equipped with heavy duty shocks and I believe that any motorist who drives a great deal, should consider this. A great deal of emphasis has been placed on horsepower and engine ad-

Careful checking of all components is a must before starting hazardous and nerve wracking tests. Loose components can cause serious damage and injuries.

Jimmy Reece liked the new Ford and chose it as his personal stock car for competition.

Jimmy Reece feels comfortable and at home in the new 1956 Ford.

vancement, but too many motorists overlook chassis setup. It's just as essential for safe driving.

Other than the carburetor slushing on the turns, the engine performed very well on the highway. That slushing, incidentally, is something that doesn't show up on dynamometer tests. Our test car, for instance, indicated 127 hp at the rear wheels at 4000 rpm, which was great. But dynos don't always show little flaws produced by road or track tests. That's another reason why stock car racing has aided automotive engineering in recent years.

The engine, with 9.25 to 1 compression, had ample torque on the highway. It never seemed to run out of rpms, and on the top speed test over a flat level road, the speedometer needle disappeared, out of sight of the 110 mph indicator. This was impressive to me because of the manner in which it jumped to a touch of the throttle. Top speed on a similar

car, without the power pack, was slightly more than 105 mph.

The first test run over the Willow Springs course was for familiarization. I had seen the track but never had driven it until making this Speed Age test. It is an impressive and rugged course, covering two and one-half miles over eleven turns that twist both left and right. The surface is almost like asphalt, although it is called a hard oil surface according to the builders. Two days of heavy rain and floods left the surface a bit greasy, but not dangerous for running.

The car was equipped with stock tires, that is, it did not have Firestone racing tires such as we would normally use for racing on a course like Willow Springs. Nor was there a safety belt in the car, which would have been a great help in holding me in a proper driving position through the sharp turns. On the second lap, I began the test for handling and per-

formance.

The first turn, leading into a sharp right hand bend after leaving the long straightaway, caused more carburetor slushing and I was able to get full power for a moment as the car leaned into the curve. I tried pumping the throttle but this was of little help, and it wasn't until the car was pointed nearly straight again that the engine put out full power. By this time, I had reached the first S turn on a steep uphill run, and shifted into second gear.

At the top of the course, the track makes a horseshoe turn and begins a sharp descent which leads into another S turn. It was here, that I discovered the steering, although fast for highway travel, was not quite fast enough for racing purposes. I moved into the first part of the turn at approximately 75 mph, which was a bit fast for this particular turn. Negotiating the left hand bend, I could feel the rear wheels begin to

Jimmy examines the Ford V-8 powerplant before starting his test runs. He was impressed and critical of its performance.

Taking care to adjust the Ford safety belt before starting his runs, Jimmy settles into the spacious cockpit.

lose traction and I cranked hard on the wheel again, but to no avail. The car spun sharply to the right and slid off the course into the dirt where I brought it to a stop without damage.

I believe that racing tires, plus faster steering would have helped in this case. Of course, I had subjected the car to racing conditions and probably took the turn faster than it should have been taken; but the two items mentioned, would have helped a great deal.

With the exception of the first turn, the engine performed well on every part of the track. Handling qualities, however, could have been much better. On one S turn, in particular, I could feel the right rear wheel lift slightly as the car leaned to the left and vice versa. At another point, on an uphill pull under full power, the front end pushed quite excessively due to the weight being shifted to the rear.

On the less critical turns, the car drifted well and held steady as I brought it straight again and headed into the straightaways. This was especially prominent on the last turn which tends to tighten more and more as you get into it and finally come out, sideways, onto the main straightaway. The sticking qualities were so good here, in fact, that I barely had to lift my foot from the throttle. I drove most of the course with brake and throttle which gives better control on a race track.

During the entire test period, I experienced no sign of brake fade, even though the binders had been punished a great deal in the turns. The entire braking system, in fact, was good. It took very little pressure to put them into operation, which is a critical point with me.

Acceleration tests following several laps to test the car's handling ability, were surprising. First, we ran the entire course for speed and came up with a lap in two minutes, 9 seconds. My slide rule tells me that this is in the neighborhood of 70-71 mph. Considering stock shocks and tires, this was fast. I do believe, however, that a correction of the carburetor slushing and racing tires would have knocked at least three seconds from this time.

My first attempt at running an acceleration test from 0 to 30 mph ended in much wheel spinning without getting anywhere. Trying for a quick start, I tromped the throttle and let out on the clutch, but the rear wheels merely spun. I finally discovered that this could be eliminated by easing the clutch out, then mashing the foot feed. The result was a 0 to 30 mph reading, in low gear, of 3.4 seconds.

The next test was 0 to 50 mph and for this one, I shifted into second at approximately 35 mph. The stop watch gave us a reading of 7.2 seconds. All of this, of course, was based on the speedometer reading. Our

1956 FORD FAIRLANE

0-30	4.4
0-50	8.4
0-60	10.2
Top Speed	109 mph

SPECIFICATIONS

Cylinders	V-8
Horsepower	200
Carburetor	4-barrel
Displacement	292 cu. in.

Test car courtesy of Dick Allen, Pomona, California.

Jimmy tools the Ford hard as he checks handling as it would be during a stock car race. His personal selection for stock car racing is the Ford.

final acceleration test was the jump from 0 to 60 and the car covered this in nine seconds flat. To be sure, we made the test five times and got the same answer. At one time, we actually beat the nine seconds reading by a fraction.

Generally, the car seemed readily adaptable for track racing. The engine seemed healthy enough with the power pack and, with the exception of carburetion in the turns, should be suitable for racing. Chassis would be the big problem. For my particular needs, I would want better shocking, of course, and a heavier sway bar for more control. Faster steering, too, would be a necessity.

Vision is good through the wide, wrap-around windshield, which is great for racing—helps you spot trouble quicker and easier. There is plenty of head room inside, even for a tall man, and the seat adjusts for plenty of comfort and leg room.

Getting back to highway driving, the throttle seems to have the necessary punch when you need it, even at 65 or 70 mph when many cars are nearly out of RPMs. The car seemed to run smooth, without effort or strain, and it flattened out the hills with comparative ease.

Our Ford test car was a 1956 Fairlane with stick transmission, and overdrive. Basically, this is the same model I will be driving in competition this season only without the overdrive. Finding a Fairlane with a stick shift can be a problem since most of them are coming through with Fordomatic, but they are available on special order and it usually takes a few weeks for delivery.

The particular car we used for our test belonged to an enthusiast named Dick Allen who keeps the automobile tuned like a fine watch. He told me earlier that he waited six weeks for delivery on his car. I've found that delivery schedules vary on these models, however, and some owners have received theirs in a matter of two weeks.

We chose the Fairlane because it was similar to the models being used in track competition. It was a two-door Club Sedan with the new 202 hp Thunderbird Y-8 engine, boasting a 292 cubic inch displacement, 8.0 to 1 compression and a four-barrel Double Twin Jet carburetor. For best possible performance on the test, we used high-test gasoline. Before the test, Dick Allen, the owner, told me that the car had been put through the drag strip at Pomona, Calif., with an average speed of 84.31 mph for the standing quarter-mile run. It was strictly stock, including the shocks, but well tuned.

Upon entering the car, I was initially and greatly impressed with the interior. The car contained Ford's new safety package A, which consists of seat belts for the driver and front seat passenger; foam rubber padded dash; and padded sun visors. A second safety package, package B, is also available and this is the same as the other but without the safety belts.

The padded dash forms a hood over the closely grouped instrument panel which prevents windshield glare from lighted instruments at night. And I was impressed with the location of the radio speaker which is set into the top of the dash and reflects the sound throughout the car. Radio knobs, however, protruded quite far from the center of the dash and I wondered how the designers overlooked this would-be hazard in their safety-minded planning. The ash tray also could have been better located. It closes into the padded dash, but there is not sufficient clearance to prevent the possibility of burn-marking the padding when a cigarette is snubbed.

Now for performance. As mentioned, the test car was equipped with overdrive and I experimented with this on the 88-mile haul to the Willow

Springs track. I decided that th definitely was not adaptable for ra ing, although it helped economy great deal. With the overdrive e gaged, the car performed well bu appeared lazy on the punch fro 60 mph on up. The needle on th speedometer climbed to 110 mp without strain, but still it seemed bit sluggish and the difference wa evident when I disengaged the ove drive lever. Still we did more tha hold our own against other cars o standing start acceleration. Top spee with overdrive, taking the speedome ter needle up slowly so as not to kic it out of overdrive, was 120 accord ing to the speedometer, as compare to the Chevvy's 110 with power pac and 105 without "goodies." The For handled well at that speed and th engine seemed to perform free an easy although conditions made it im possible for too long a run.

Without overdrive, the differenc was tremendous. On acceleration u to 90 mph, the car was virtuall poison. Top speed was not as hig as with the overdrive, but the punc was better and more suited to comp tition requirements. Over a course one-mile, indicated on the odomete the engine peaked out at 109 mph i high gear.

Second gear acceleration was be ter, too, and the needle swung shar ly up to 84 mph before peaking ou Experimenting with gear ratio prob ably would have helped in this r spect and in the track test which w made later.

The ride generally was smooth an comfortable, as was the Chevrol tested a week earlier. On the highwa to Willow Springs, we used norm air pressure, but for the track test I insisted upon 40 pounds in eac tire. The tires, by the way, were stoc tubeless, and the increase in pressur helps prevent "roll-over" on the edg while cornering sharply on a trac

On the highway, I had one com plaint on steering which I believ came from lack of proper front en alignment. Even in easy turns, ther seemed to be a bind in the wheel an the car did not recover as quickly I would prefer. The Chevrolet in th respect, was quick recovering an fast steering.

Brakes held solidly enough, b there was a bad chattering when the were applied under heavy pressur and this was due to the drums bein out of round. They needed to turned and centered for best perform ance. The owner told me that th condition had existed in the car sinc he took delivery, but his dealer a sured him that the condition woul be fixed.

My chief criticism on all stock production cars also applied in the case of the Ford—it definitely is under-shocked for heavy travel! I think most race drivers are more conscious of this feeling than the average driver since we are in contact with this situation almost constantly.

I was more used to the two and one-half mile road racing course at Willow Springs this time. On previous tests I was able to pick out shut off and shifting points, so it was not like driving a strange track for the first time. After feeling the car out on the highway, I was anxious to see just how it reacted on the track.

I made two laps at fair speeds to get even better acquainted with both car and track. It appeared to handle very well and the car's sticking qualities let me know that I could go into those eleven left and right hand turns considerably fast, without getting into trouble. It had been rather more difficult with the Chevvy.

My first search for defects was in the extremely sharp first turn which begins a slow upward pull. I concentrated on engine performance and found no ill effects. Through the tight corner, where shifting of weight can cause carburetion slosh and flat spots (as it did in the Chevrolet), the engine ran good. I noticed no cutting out or lag as I applied more throttle.

Nearing the top of the upgrade, which becomes steeper and leads into a sharp ascent through a tight left hand bend requiring use of second gear, I could feel the right rear wheel lift slightly from the force of the curve. However, the car remained stable and moved through the turn with not too great a lean.

Leveling off at the top of the course and heading downhill to a treacherous S turn, I knew this would be a real handling test, for I had spun in this spot with the Chevrolet the week before and other cars also were reported to have trouble with this turn. We hit it, still in second gear which helped break our speed from approximately 75 mph, twisted through the right hand turn and quickly back to the left. Coming out I pulled the lever into high gear and we sailed through a slight straightaway, picking up speed as we approached the ever tightening and tricky last turn. We hit this at 100-mph and our speed dropped only slightly through it, before picking up top speed on the long main chute.

The safety belts were a great help on a course such as Willow Springs where the turns are tight and come at you quickly. Without a belt, it is more difficult to maintain a good driving position. I think this applies to highway driving also.

I tried for lap speed and we came away with a 2 minute, 7.6 second clocking for the full lap, which was surprising. With the Chevvy, I did a lap in two minutes, nine seconds. I believe the car, with its sticking characteristics in the corners, could have been extended further for a better lap speed. Again, shocks with proper stiffness would have helped a great deal and racing tires also would have made a difference.

For actual handling performance, the car worked very well as did the engine. In the turns, the Ford didn't lean exceptionally and it went into an easy side drift, sticking there with a stable feeling. Probably the chassis could have handled even more power from the engine. The Chevrolet was slightly less effective on the twins.

I was especially impressed with handling through the big bend leading onto the main straightaway. It's rather sharp, although it doesn't look it until you actually get into it too hot and find yourself in trouble. It gives one the illusion that it is about to straighten out when actually it is bending tighter. But the car seemed to work better through here on each lap and I believe it could have handled the turn at full power without too much trouble.

Brake fade during the runs was noticeable but not great. It became more prominent in acceleration tests, with frequent quick stops. Chatter from the drums being out of round was very prominent on all quick stops, and especially during lap tests where the brakes were used along with the throttle through the turns. The Chevrolet was better, in the department, showing no brake fade during the entire test.

We ran a series of acceleration tests, using stop watches and the speedometer. For accuracy, we covered each range five times or more for a good average. The first was run from 0 to 30, and the Fairlane clicked this off in 4.41 seconds. The 0 to 40 with a 6.21 second reading, and the check took a bit longer of course, 0 to 50 tests gave us an 8.41 second answer. The final test, from 0 to 60, ticked off 10.21 seconds.

The acceleration tests were rather difficult to make with accuracy, since the rear wheels broke loose or slipped on the initial take-off which indicated plenty of power. In all cases, where shifting was necessary, the shifting point was approximately 35 mph. We did get one 0 to 60 reading at 9.41 seconds but our average was 10.21 as mentioned.

Quite frankly, I was more impressed with the Ford after putting it through a test over the road racing course at Willow Springs. And, quite frankly again, I chose to ride a Ford in competition this season long before I ran either test for SPEED AGE.

JIMMY REECE

At 26, Jimmy Reece, of Oklahoma City, Oklahoma, is one of the seasoned veterans of big time racing. He will be making his fifth appearance this year at Indianapolis.

Jimmy has been racing nearly ten years and he drives them all—Indianapolis, sprints, midgets and stock cars. In the three Indy races in which he has competed Jim boasts a seventh and seventeenth. Last year, after moving up steadily through fast-moving traffic, his car was the first to be side-lined when a connecting rod ventilated the engine, and he placed 33d.

The 1954 season was his best on the Championship Trail, although it ended on a somewhat painful note. Nearing the end of the season, with a strong chance to edge Indianapolis winner Bill Vukovich for fourth place in national standings, Jimmy's car became involved in an accident that placed him in the hospital—with a broken shoulder, crushed ribs and a punctured lung. Despite this, he wound up with 1,000 National Championship points to tie Vukie for fourth spot.

Signed to drive a new car at Indianapolis this year, Jim also plans to campaign the Championship Trail, sprints, midgets and the stockers. •

'57 CHEVROLET

. . . chalks up another first with production fuel injection
or your choice of six other engine options

by Walt Woron

WHAT GIVES THE CHEVY V8 ITS HORSEPOWER?

	CU. IN.	COMPRESSION RATIO	CARBURETION	DUAL EXHAUSTS	OTHER
162	265	8 to 1	2-Barrel	No	——
185	283	8.5 to 1	2-Barrel	No	——
220	283	9.5 to 1	4-Barrel	Yes	——
245	283	9.5 to 1	Two 4-Barrel	Yes	——
250	283	9.5 to 1	Fuel Injection	Yes	——
270	283	9.5 to 1	Two 4-Barrel	Yes	Special Camshaft
283	283	10.5 to 1	Fuel Injection	Yes	Special Camshaft

"YOU'VE GOT TO GET UP off the canvas before you can start swinging." With this facetious remark, Chevrolet's General Manager, Ed Cole, has thrown down the gauntlet to Ford. It's apparent that he thinks such improvements as fuel injection, smoother power transition from engine to driveshaft, a variety of V8 engines, and an accomplished face-lifting job on the '56 body will be enough to keep the competition from swinging too hard. Let's analyze these changes so you can make your own decision.

Engine

Do you want practically *any* horsepower from 162 to 283 in your Chevy V8? You name it, they've got it. Two size V8s are available, one the same size (265 cubic inches) as last year, and another one that's been bored ⅛-inch to 3.875 to increase its displacement to 283 inches. Outside of the increased bore (stroke remains the same three inches), power is upped by various combinations of raised compression ratios, higher lift (0.398) camshafts, four barrel carburetion, dual four-barrels, and fuel injection (see Engine Chart, page 26).

Outside of these changes, other refinements to the block and accessories have been made: 1) Full pressure lubrication is used to the valve lifters instead of the former metered system. 2) Mechanical lifters are used in engines that have fuel injection and compression ratios up to 10.5 to one. 3) Top deck of the V8 block has been increased in thickness to minimize cylinder wall distortion through overtightening of the head hold-down bolts. 4) Spark plugs have longer reach and metal heat deflection shields to protect the wires and boots from the heat of the exhaust manifold. 5) Gas passages gradually increase in cross-sectional area in the inlet ports and in the exhaust manifold, for better scavenging and more volumetric efficiency. 6) A new distributor with breaker points directly above the shaft

Cutaway front view of the 283-cubic-inch Chevy engine discloses the relative locations and operation of the various components in action.

bearing is used to reduce fluctuations in the gap setting. 7) Front and intermediate bearings are ¹⁄₁₆-inch thicker.

Fuel Injection

The much-publicized and little understood fuel injection system will be available as standard equipment on Corvette engines, but can also be had on the big V8 powering any other Chevrolet car. Basically designed by General Motors Staff Engineering and built by Rochester Products, the system was simplified somewhat by a Chevrolet engineering team headed up by Chief Engineer Harry Barr, using the talents of such men as Zora Arkus-Duntov, famous designer of the Ardun head.

Basically, Chevrolet's fuel injection system consists of three components: fuel meter, manifold assembly, and air meter. Together these units replace the normal carburetor and intake manifold. Instead of fuel and air being pre-mixed in a carburetor, then being forced through intake manifolding to each cylinder, the air supply is taken in separately through a manifold. The fuel is injected directly and constantly into each intake port, where the two then mix.

The advantages of such a system over the normal carburetor system, as noted by Rochester Products and Chevrolet engineers, are: More overall fuel economy resulting from better volumetric efficiency due to fuel cut-off while decelerating; fast starting and faster warmup during cold weather; more power (about five more hp than a comparable Chevy engine with two four-barrel carbs); elimination of carburetor or manifold icing; and a reduction in stalling tendencies caused by taking turns too quickly or making sudden stops.

The basic operation of the system is as follows: Air is fed to the air meter and is metered past a throttle valve—controlled by the position of the accelerator—into the manifold passages which feed each cylinder. As the air flows through the air meter, a signal is transmitted to the fuel meter, which determines the proper amount of fuel to be fed to the cylinders. The fuel is pumped to eight nozzles, one each in the manifold passage just above the intake valve. There the fuel and air mix and enter the cylinder when the intake valve opens. **continued**

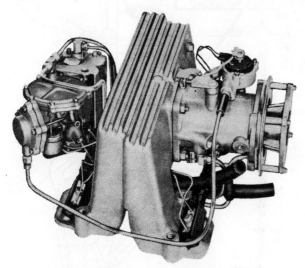

The complete fuel injection setup looks like this before installation.

CHEVROLET '57

continued

' To follow through the operation in detail, refer to the schematic. When the accelerator pedal is pushed down, the throttle valve (A) is opened, admitting air into the intake manifold. At the same time a signal is sent to the fuel meter so that the air/fuel mixture will be in the proper ratio. Fuel to the system is supplied by a conventional engine fuel pump, flows through a filter to a fuel bowl (B), controlled by a float system similar to those used in carburetors. The high pressure fuel pump (C), driven by a cable from the distributor, pumps the fuel under pressure to the fuel control valve (D).

This valve is fundamentally the metering device of the fuel injection system, for through a system of controls tied to it, it determines the amount of fuel that is pumped to the engine. In almost all operation, except wide-open throttle, some of the fuel is bypassed and allowed to return to the fuel bowl. The amount of fuel that spills back into the fuel bowl determines the pressure within the fuel valve, which in turn depends on the position of the spill plunger.

For starting, a solenoid (E) connected to the starter circuit operates to unseat the fuel valve and allow fuel flow past the valve to the nozzles (F) at cranking rpm. When the fuel valve returns to normal, all fuel flows through the center of the valve. There is a ball check in the valve that prevents fuel flow until

there is sufficient pressure to condense any vapor in the system.

During warmup, the necessary rich mixtures are provided by blocking the vacuum passage to the enrichment diaphragm (G). This is done by a ball check in the electric choke (H) that remains closed until the coil is heated sufficiently to force a piston to unseat it.

During idling, when the airflow is so low that it has little effect on the fuel control diaphragm (J), the venturi signal is strengthened by manifold vacuum through a tube to the enrichment diaphragm. This can be manually adjusted by a needle valve, one of the two manual adjustments possible in this system—the other being for increasing or decreasing the amount of fuel. At idling speeds, 40 per cent of the air enters the system through air galleries at each fuel nozzle.

When decelerating, a spring-loaded diaphragm (coasting shutoff diaphragm, K) reacts to closed-throttle deceleration vacuum to lift a valve in the high pressure pump outlet, which completely relieves pump pressure so that there is no fuel flow.

One of the keys to the success of this system is the design of the fuel nozzles. Instead of discharging directly to vacuum, they discharge to atmospheric pressure and the spray (at pressures up to 200 psi) is targeted across an air duct into the manifold just above the intake port. This allows larger orifices

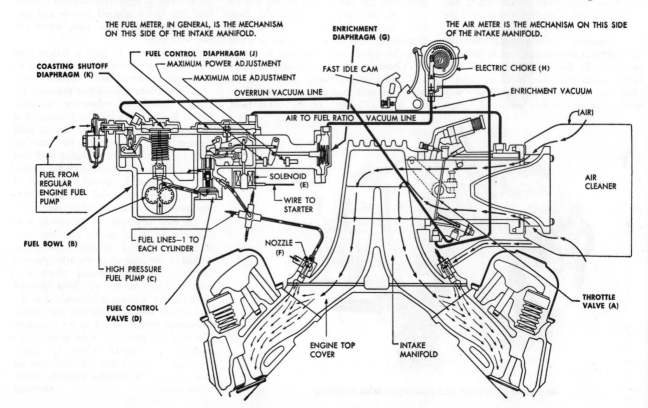

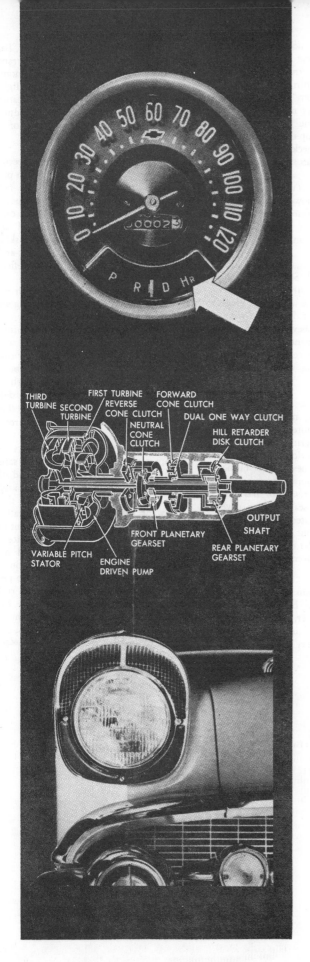

THIRD TURBINE · SECOND TURBINE · FIRST TURBINE · REVERSE CONE CLUTCH · FORWARD CONE CLUTCH · NEUTRAL CONE CLUTCH · DUAL ONE WAY CLUTCH · HILL RETARDER DISK CLUTCH · OUTPUT SHAFT · FRONT PLANETARY GEARSET · REAR PLANETARY GEARSET · VARIABLE PITCH STATOR · ENGINE DRIVEN PUMP

(0.011-inch), reduces fuel percolation due to vacuum in the fuel lines, and allows a continuous fuel flow at low rpms.

In general, servicing problems should be minor, particularly if the proper factory machining and settings have been made. The only electrical part of the system that could cause trouble would be the solenoid; everything else operates mechanically. If any dirt does manage to slip by the 10-micron fuel filter between the two fuel pumps and the even more efficient filter in the plunger, and then proceeds to partially clog one of the nozzles, the remedy is simple. You take an open-end wrench to remove the nozzle, blow it out with air, and reinstall it. The eight nozzles come in sets, and if one is damaged it is replaced with one of the same coding from another set.

Transmissions

The manual three-speed transmission still remains the basic transmission for the '57 Chevrolet, with overdrive as an optional extra. Also available on the six and 265-V8 is Powerglide; on the bigger V8, you can get the new Turboglide.

Mechanically, Turboglide consists of three turbines and two planetary gearsets, combined with a variable pitch stator and the conventional torque converter pump, all enclosed in a die-cast aluminum housing (lighter by 82 pounds than last year's Powerglide). In very simple terms, the forward motion is obtained by the oil in the torque converter rotating one of three turbines in succession, which start rotating dependent on the position of their respective vanes. As the turning force of one of the turbines lessens, another takes over to maintain a constant positive drive with no apparent "shifting."

When the quadrant is positioned at D (its only forward position) and the engine is running, oil is pumped into the converter by the engine-driven pump (see cutaway). The first turbine starts to rotate, driving its shaft and the output shaft through the rear planetary gearset. When it reaches a certain speed the second turbine starts to rotate, in turn driving the front planetary gearset and the output shaft. Next, the third turbine starts rotating, turning its shaft that is directly connected to the transmission output shaft. Eventually, all three turbines are free-wheeling.

When the throttle is floor-boarded for passing, the variable pitch stator comes into play, increasing its blade angle and delivering greater torque to the output shaft.

HR on the quadrant stands for HILL RETARDER, which takes the position (not the function) of LOW on Powerglide. It is used strictly for what its name implies—slowing you down when you're going downhill. Since it operates by creating a turbulence in the oil of the torque converter to impart a drag on the rear wheels, it is of no value for low-gear acceleration.

Chassis

Changes in the '57 chassis are minor, with wheelbase remaining at 115 inches, but overall length being increased to 16 feet, 8 inches. Chevrolet has followed the move to 14-inch, lower pressure (22 psi) tires. There are slight modifications to the front suspension and shocks, while the rear outrigger springs have been moved further outboard for the purpose of getting better handling.

Body

Styling changes in the face-lifted '56 bodies are accompanied by an increased windshield glass area (from 69 to 75 more square inches) resulting from the lowered hoodline, and a new ventilation system. Air for the passenger compartment is taken in through intake screens over each headlight, reaching it through louvered outlets at either edge of the dash panel.

A total of 460 model-color combinations (up 96 over last year), 17 exterior colors (seven new ones) with 16 solid and 15 two-tone combinations, and a statement by General Manager Ed Cole that "It will take more than styling to sell cars (in '57)" just about tells the '57 Chevrolet story—except for driving it,

Chevrolet Road Test

CONTINUED FROM PAGE 56

nearly as far as the other seatback, a nice detail. (Basically, this keeps seat from hitting steering wheel, also discourages passengers from flattening the driver against the steering wheel when they get out on the left.)

Hardtop headroom is 2 inches less than in 4-door sedans, but lack of space isn't too noticeable until you're forced to the sloping outer edge by a pair of husky passengers. There's no decrease in hip-room, no noticeable loss of shoulder room. Surroundings are pleasant; bolsters and facings (top, front edge of cushions) are vinyl, as are headlining, door panel trim.

ECONOMY AND EASE OF MAINTENANCE

Fuel economy: Not damaged by new power (as it has been in 225-hp job). Results from last year compare closely to '56 figures; shows improvement at 30, 45 mph which may be insignificant due to differences in engines, transmission, tune, other factors beyond our test controls. But more noticeable increase in economy at 60 can indicate efficiency of new cam at mid-speed rpms. (Valve size and intake ports are not changed to accommodate better breathing offered by higher-lifting camshaft.)

Our traffic checks, run over a more true-to-life course than last year (but still under controlled conditions for accuracy), show a decrease in mileage; but as we suspected after steady-speed and traffic tests were completed, the new car struck a good balance as shown by the tank average, a balance substantiated by Chevrolet's remarks on what they designed into the car—performance, with no sacrifice in fuel economy.

Is the car well put together? We've found from past experience that Chevrolet construction varies no more between cheap models and deluxe hardtops than 2 Bel Airs would vary from each other. Test car had good-fitting body panels, hood and decklid. From what we could see of the new gas filler mechanism (you turn a vertical chrome bar above the left tail light lens to drop the light housing and expose the filler neck), there should be no unusual troubles with the latch, spring or hinge.

Interior appointments (upholstery, door-panels, floor mats) showed good fit, no gaps or wrinkles; windshield trim molding joined well at edges of wraparound, fit of glove compartment and ashtray doors passed our inspection.

How did it hold up? Space for "Items that go wrong on car during test" in our road test form drew a complete blank. (We listened closely for drive train whine found in another '56 Chevy driven a short time before the test, but noticed no moans from test car's running gear, no clunks in Powerglide transmission when upshifting or downshifting.)

Servicing: Most engine components remain where they were, most are easy to get to. But perhaps more important, because of some engineering changes, you may get even better service from your V8 in '56. Generator has new rubber-bushed mountings to reduce noise and vibration. New model's voltage regulator has been waterproofed (rubber seal between cover and base), is now located on left fender skirt instead of up front on the radiator baffle (this lets Chevrolet use shorter wires, makes unit easier, and accordingly cheaper, to service).

Other electrical system changes include waterproofing neoprene boot over starter motor solenoid plunger, fuse in main light switch to protect instrument panel light circuit, new battery (rubber separators instead of wood, new grid alloy, baffles in the vent caps) with a warranty period of 3 years instead of 55's 21-month period. Chevrolet's new-type headlights (detailed in December '55 MT) feature 3-point aiming system for quick adjustment, low-beam visibility increase of as much as 80 feet.

Summing up: Hidden engineering changes in '56 interested us more than pros and cons of styling changes. (In fact, we've heard so much comment on Chevy's new grille and side molding that we can't tell what the majority thinks of the changeover. Did find many people asking if rear fenders were peaked or if paint-and-chrome of Bel Airs achieved the effect; it's the latter.)

But taking away the glitter (which you can do in varying degrees by selecting any number of models), you come up with a car highly impressive in performance, a genuine pleasure to drive, and a car with mechanical features that point up low-cost, long-term ownership. (And so no buyer will have to live with a too-drab machine, Chevy has initiated what may be a definite trend by dolling up its plainest 150 series with side trim and chrome around the windshield.)

Chevrolet is playing what appears like an unpretentious role in the Detroit safety show; dash covering, seatbelts, and the shoulder harness setup in particular aren't being pushed, but they're there for those who want them; safety-type doorlatches were installed in '55s (in July), went unannounced. In power and performance, in appearance and trade-in value, and now safety, Chevy is keeping competition on its toes, might even step on a few to keep from being trampled in the '56 sales rush; they've added new features to the cars, added more cars to the line, and thrown a potent package onto the low-price-class bargain table labeled "Hot." —**Jim Lodge**

Side view of '57 Chevy Two-Ten four-door hardtop shows new sweeping spear molding, hooded headlamps, rear fender fins. Note new hubcaps.

Bel Air convertible sports new aluminum trim panel on finned rear fender. All '57 models have new lower grille and twin ornaments.

CHEVROLET HAS GONE all-out to win the 1957 lap of the horsepower race in the low-price field. Chevy's top-of-the-line "Corvette" V8 (available on all models) turns up a walloping 283 bhp—58 bhp more than the '56 line's most powerful engine.

Power increases stem from ⅛-inch bore increase, higher lift camshafts, multiple carburetion or—surprise of the year—fuel injection! The 283 bhp fuel-injection engine (Chevy calls it Ramjet), turns up one horsepower per cubic inch of displacement.

Other engines offered are: a 140 bhp six, a 265 cu. in. V8 of 162 bhp and versions of the 283 cu. in. engine developing 185, 220, 245, 250, and 270 bhp.

A brand new automatic transmission called "Turboglide" is optional on all 283 cu. in. engines. This new automatic consists of three torque converter turbines combined with a variable pitch stator and two planetary gearsets.

The entire front end, side panels and rear fenders have been restyled for '57. Chassis changes include 14-inch wheels, shock absorber and rear spring modifications. ●

Cutaway of Chevrolet's 283 cu. in. engine shows details of Ramjet fuel injection system. Air enters intake manifold through cleaner at upper right while fuel is sprayed continuously at 200 lbs. per square inch pressure from nozzles at each intake port (left center).

DRIVING A FUEL INJECTION
CHEVROLET

Since Chevrolet is now giving us the first U.S. volume-production system of fuel injection, the practical benefits can now be measured from behind the wheel:

- ● Is there any big improvement in acceleration?

- ● What's the throttle action like?

- ● Can a driver tell the difference between cars equipped with fuel injection and normal carburetors?

- ● Does fuel injection work better in hard turns?

- ● How about smoothness—and starting?

BY KEN FERMOYLE

THE 1957 MODEL introduction season was expected to provide a lot of surprises. It did, and the most surprising development of all was the introduction of fuel injection by Chevrolet.

What caught just about everyone, in and out of the industry, off guard was the fact that Chevrolet came out with injection on an across-the-board basis. There had been speculation that some form of fuel injection *might* be offered for Corvettes, but not even the wildest rumors included standard passenger cars in on the deal!

As we all know now, however, all four Corvette V-8s—two with carburetors, two with injection—have been made available *as options for passenger car use.*

So much for background; what everyone is waiting to find out is what it's like to *drive* Chevrolets equipped with fuel injection.

I was one of the fortunate people who found out early. I drove a number of new Chevrolets—some passenger cars, some Corvettes; some with fuel injection, some with carburetors; some with new Turboglide transmissions, some with Powerglide or stick shifts—before and just after the new models were announced.

There's no outward evidence to tip you off to whether or not a new Chevrolet has f.i. or carbs. There's none of the characteristic whistle you get with superchargers, for example.

There *are* some important differences which show up when you're behind the wheel, with your foot on the throttle.

Most obvious is the instantaneous response you get when you ask for it. Mash the throttle down and you're gone right now! There isn't a slight hesitation or the lag you often find with carburetor engines. That, of course, is because the fuel charge is lying right in the injector nozzle in the intake port just waiting for the valve to open.

Another thing you will probably notice when you first drive a Chevrolet with fuel injection is that there isn't any coughing, sputtering or momentary loss of power when you take a fairly tight turn at a rapid clip. This often occurs under similar conditions in cars with carburetors, due to temporary fuel starvation.

The angle of the car has no effect on fuel injection engines, however. Gasoline isn't sloshing around in the float chamber and depending on gravity and manifold pressure alone to get it thru the carburetor, manifold passages and intake ports. It's under pressure supplied by a gear pump.

One thing that surprised me slightly was the fact that you could slow down to just above idling speed in high gear, then floor the accelerator and take off smoothly with no bucking. I had heard in the past that low speed, high gear operation was one of the problems plaguing engineers. You certainly couldn't complain about Chevrolet's f.i. system in this respect, however.

I didn't have a chance to run performance checks on a Chevrolet passenger sedan equipped with the injection engine, but I did hold a watch on a Corvette with injectors. The results were little short of amazing.

First thing I did was make a series of runs from 0-60 mph. (We had previously checked speedometer error by timing the car thru a measured course at a steady, indicated 60 mph, since we did not have a chance to use the fifth wheel.)

A number of 0-60 runs in opposite directions averaged out at 6.8 seconds! The fastest was 6.7 seconds!

This was impressive, but I'm convinced that the car could have done even *better.* Big problem was to get away without wheelspin—and some practice undoubtedly would have taught us just the point to which you can rev the engine before popping the clutch without breaking traction. I know I was able to improve times with the carburetor-equipped '56 Corvette I tested last year after I had experimented awhile.

At any rate, the way the Corvette took off was, literally, breath-taking. And it didn't quit at 60 mph, either. Several 0-80 mph runs netted an average of 11.3 seconds—pretty fair 0-60 time for most cars. The fastest of these runs was just a shade over 11 seconds flat.

Next on the agenda was a check of 50-80 mph times. All these runs were made in second gear. (Previous acceleration checks were made using first and second only, since the Corvette was equipped with the close-ratio, three-speed manual transmission which permits use of second to very high points in the speed range.) The average for these was 4.95 seconds. There was practically no variation in times in this case; all were either 4.9 or 5.0 seconds.

It's worth mentioning that all '57 Chevrolets I've driven so far have had remarkably little speedometer error. They've averaged just about two miles slow at 60 and you hit an actual 80 at about the 85 mark on the dial.

In studying the performance figures mentioned, it should be noted that the Corvette tested had the 250-hp V-8. There are two hotter engines available, along with another of 245 hp. The latter, which has a single four-barrel carburetor, is like the 250-hp V-8 in that both use hydraulic valve lifters.

They also use a cam with a milder grind than the two higher-powered engines. In fact, Chevrolet engineers refer to them as the "street engines" among themselves. The 270- and 283-hp V-8s are called "competition engines."

The 270-hp job has twin four-barrel carburetors. The 283-hp V-8 has fuel injection and a 10.5-to-1 compression ratio. (All of the other three have 9.5-to-1 ratios.) This, the hottest of the "hot ones," is a really high-winding engine. It doesn't develop maximum horsepower until it hits *6000 rpm!*

I haven't had an opportunity to run fuel consumption checks on any 1957 Chevrolet—fuel injection or carburetor—as yet. So, I can't tell you what f.i. does in this respect. Chevrolet has purposely refrained from making any extravagant claims in this direction. One reason was they hadn't had time to complete exhaustive testing themselves. However, I talked to one engineer not long before this was written and he said results of tests to date have been a pleasant surprise.

There was only one slight blot on my experience with Chevrolet's fuel injection. After completing acceleration checks with the Corvette, I pulled off the track to make some notes. I stalled the engine accidentally—and we had a little difficulty getting it started again. Fuel injection is supposed to eliminate vapor lock, but it seemed like that was the trouble. Maybe it was just flooded, however. I'm not that much of an expert on f.i. that I could say for sure. At any rate, we finally got started again in five or 10 minutes.

One question that has been asked repeatedly since Chevrolet announced that it would offer injection for '57 is: "How reliable will it be? Will the continuous flow system used be practical for day-to-day use?"

The answer to that will have to wait, obviously. Until a number of Chevrolets with injection units have been on the road for awhile, there's no way of telling. Certainly the brief time I spent behind the wheel wasn't enough to tell.

If there's one thing that Chevrolet has been noted for thru the years, however, it's reliability. In fact, there was little else to recommend the make to the performance-minded for many years. So, it's hard to picture the company coming out with a feature it didn't feel would hold up in the type of service it will be subjected to, in all situations.

Certainly a lot of respected engineers who helped develop Chevrolet's fuel injection system feel it will get the job done —and with a minimum of fuss or trouble. A normal quota of bugs may crop up, as with any radically new automotive development, however. We'll just have to wait and see.

Another question heard a lot concerns the availability of fuel injection, either on Corvettes or Chevrolet passenger cars.

Theoretically, of course, you can get the system on *any* 1957 Chevrolet product (barring trucks). Practically, no evidence could be found of any being sold with f.i. as this was written. Could have happened, but not so far as we know.

When fuel injection Chevrolets do start to appear in any quantity, it's my guess that the bulk of them will have the 250-hp engines. (It looks also like the first f.i. models out will be Corvettes—which is only natural.) Cars with the 283-hp V-8 might prove rather hard to get for the average buyer. And probably won't be what the average buyer will want anyhow. Their hot cams, with attendant rough idle and relatively poor low-speed performance, make them better suited for competition or high-speed touring than normal driving.

The same is true, to some extent, for the dual four-barrel, 270-hp engines. Actually the performance of either of these hotter engines will be little, if any, better in the more commonly used ranges than the 250- or 245-hp Corvette engines. Acceleration under 60 mph probably won't be noticeably better.

There's one point about Chevrolet's fuel injection that hasn't been cleared up at this date. That is the one about just what the system will cost. At this writing, no official price has been announced, although most other prices are out.

There have been many guesses, however. Guesses ranging from "about $90" to "in the neighborhood of $300." One of the most reliable of many "informed sources" has set the figure at $190. That sounds reasonable, but is still only a guess. Chevrolet brass may not even know for certain. This is something else we'll just have to wait for.

Since we're talking about questions that have come up concerning Chevrolet's fuel injection system, there's another one that might be mentioned. Some people have wondered just *why* Chevrolet elected to introduce it for 1957—and how long ago the decision to do so was made.

It isn't hard to figure out why. Chevrolet's important competitors all made major model changeovers, and it was common knowledge a long time ago that they were planning to do just that. Chevrolet, on the other hand, had decided to go the major facelift route for '57.

This meant Chevrolet couldn't expect to draw as much attention as, say, Ford and Plymouth. Both are all-new cars. What better way to equalize the situation than to drop an unexpected bombshell like fuel injection?

When did Chevrolet decide to take the step? That's hard to pin down, but there is evidence the decision was a last-minute one in auto industry terms. Best guess is that plans to introduce f.i. for '57 were made just this past summer. Of course, much developmental work had gone before.

About the same time I drove the fuel injection Corvette, I had a chance to ride in a car with a totally different f.i. system. The car was a '56 Chrysler and it was equipped with the Bendix Electrojector system (pictured in Special Reports last month).

A complete departure from past fuel injection systems, the Bendix unit is unique in that it is controlled and operated by electronics. It is a timed or metered system and is the only method of injection seen yet which requires no pump drive off the engine.

My experience was rather frustrating, since I didn't have a chance to drive the car and the ride I did get was confined to Detroit streets where traffic was rather heavy. As a result, I could tell little about Electrojector's virtues or flaws.

I did notice that the characteristic f.i. instant throttle response was there. The Bendix engineer driving kicked it a couple of times and the big Chrysler took off immediately. I noticed, too, that the car started very fast before we left on our short jaunt.

It was impossible to tell how the system lugged at low speeds, because the Chrysler had an automatic transmission. There were no flat spots within the limited speed range we explored. ●

Buyers of the lowest-priced "Big Three" made 56 out of every 100 new-car purchases last year. The remaining 16 makes divided the other 44 per cent among them.

You can choose, within any Big Three make, from a variety of engines, power equipment on those engines, transmissions, bodies, interior and exterior trim, and accessories—or lack of them—that is unequalled in the high-priced lines. You'll also get handling that beats most big cars, whether on the highway or nosing into a tight parking slot.

But it'll be hard to make up your mind this year as to which of the Big Three is best. On these pages are our road tests, so now it's your move.

an MT Research Report by Pete Molson

CHEVROLET ROAD TEST

THE ONLY ONE of the Big Three to resist a complete body change is Chevrolet, and it is by far the best equipped of the lowest priced group to do so. With a more than comfortable '56 sales lead over Ford and an unbroken record of winning every sales race for more than 20 years, Chevy can complacently count on coming out ahead once more in '57.

There are many changes in the new Chevrolet, and most of them seem aimed at making the even hotter one hotter yet.

The test car, a Bel Air four-door hardtop, had a fresh look when compared with its year-old counterpart. What it may have lost in identity as a Chevrolet, it has gained in resemblance to Buick and Olds at the front and to Cadillac at the rear. Not a few Chevy fanciers will consider this similarity highly desirable.

Like many first-off-the-line cars, ours had an odd combination of equipment. The engine was the hottest of Chevy's non-fuel-injected varieties, putting out 270 horsepower and using two four-barrel carburetors, solid valve lifters, and the hot cam. Curiously coupled with this was Powerglide. Either Turboglide (not available on the earliest cars, which we were forced to choose from) or a manual shift would have given us better times in the acceleration runs. Further checks will be made later in the year with cars better broken-in, as well as more logically equipped. Important variations will be reported to you.

The test car had neither power brakes nor power steering.

How would you expect this particular Chevrolet to stack up to some of the other performance combinations available in the line? This is the hottest carburetor engine; compared with the 250-horsepower FI powerplant, or any of the other carburetor-equipped choices, this engine should give more go and less economy. Comparing Powerglide with other transmissions, it doesn't give the acceleration you'll get from the new Turboglide or from a stick shift. The stick shift has better economy than either automatic, and Turboglide's fuel mileage shouldn't differ much from that of Powerglide if you drive conservatively. That, by the way, will be hard to do.

Will It Be Best-Handling Car Again in '57?

It doesn't look that way. Retaining its ball-joint front suspension, Chevrolet has cancelled out some of its advantages by going to a somewhat softer ride, with resultant greater lean on corners, and less confidence for the driver. There is no question that the car looks and feels bigger, and we can't blame Chevy for giving in to the buying public's apparent feelings in the matter. Personally, we prefer the taut feel of the '56.

The non-power steering is easy. Except in parking, the GM power steering really isn't needed except for someone whose physical condition demands it. Chevy retains its high-mounted wheel and most drivers will sit high, as in the Ford.

The instruments are newly mounted in a higher position, the cowl itself having been dropped slightly to give a newer look. (Unfortunately this made it necessary to move the fresh-air intake back to the front of the car. The "new" grilles around the headlights for this purpose are in a position that has been generally discredited because of exhaust fumes in close traffic.)

Vision is good and, we're glad to say, undistorted. An exception is the rear-view mirror, now cowl mounted. It blocks the right front fender for shorter drivers and isn't big enough to make the wrap-around rear window truly useful. The Eldorado fins help in parking.

Out on the open road, connoisseurs of handling will note the same tendency to get bigger and softer at the expense of crispness in handling. Though you won't have to fight the wheel, front-end heaviness is evident in a mushier feel. The figures show that Chevrolet has the best weight distribution among the three cars, but the driver benefits little.

Recovery to an originally straight course when the wheel is whipped from side to side is fair. A sharply crowned road demands considerable correction.

Despite these criticisms, the '57 Chevrolet remains a good car to handle. We feel that the tendency to let power outstrip the chassis has popped up here, however, and we're ag'in it.

Is It As Roadable As It Was?

It takes irregular surfaces in its stride. Normal highway dips cause it no embarrassment. When they get bad, it bounces (but doesn't bottom) and then recovers quickly with no oscillation to bother the driver.

On curves, body lean and tire squeal combine to warn you of approaching limits. You have all the necessary power to pull out if you get in trouble, but see that you stay on the pavement for sure control.

At ordinary speeds on soft or washboard roads, control is surprisingly good. Elapsed time need not suffer on back roads, and passengers will fare better than in earlier Chevrolets.

Is the Hotter One the Hottest?

There's no doubt that it still holds the title in its field. Particularly when you remember that we had a low-performance transmission, the test figures are impressive. It beat all the times of last year's powerpacked test car and all the times of the Ford and Plymouth this year except for the Plymouth's time from 0-45 mph.

Much more pleasing to us than the standing-start times are those for acceleration at passing speeds. They should, of course, not be abused by the power-happy, and quite possibly that's what will happen. Still, a car that can almost fly from 45 to 60 in a mere 2.9 seconds is one that should be capable of keeping you and your family out of trouble.

The extremely slow shift of the Powerglide transmission makes us hope that it will soon be dropped in favor of Turboglide. Rough idling can be expected from the hot camshaft in the powerpack engine.

What Has Happened to Fuel Mileage?

The steady speed consumption figures have suffered with the huge increase in power. Ordinary driving, with its conditions closer to those you might experience with your own car, yielded little change from last year's comparable car. If you want a real high-performance car this year and still have to consider your gasoline bill, we have a suggestion: learn to drive smoothly and conservatively as a general rule, saving bursts of speed or acceleration for special occasions. It's more fun that way, it will mean money in your pocket, and your passengers will be less ruffled.

How Are the Brakes?

This test car had just been born when we took it over, so we had tester Jeff Cooper take it on a leisurely trip over varying terrain to break it in. He returned it with this note attached: "Brakes are inadequate for mountain driving or highway with traffic. Fade early." Time was so short that we couldn't complete our regular tests in time for this issue. A full report will follow.

Does It Ride Better?

The ride is considerably softer than on the '55 and '56 Chevrolet. Road irregularities, from highway tar strips up

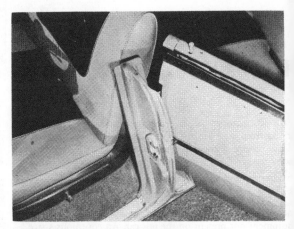

STURDY STUB post kept test car's body rigid, free from creaks and groans of many hardtops. Flush sills, washable headliner make interior easy to clean.

GIANT AIR CLEANERS conceal thirsty dual carburetors. Finger points to linkage that cuts in front carburetor when rear one needs a helping hand in acceleration.

PHOTOS BY BOB D'OLIVO

COOL ENGINE is desirable before you go changing plugs. Despite this, light and compact V8 gives remarkably shipshape engine room, an example for others to follow.

CHEVROLET ROAD TEST continued

through the tribulations of a washboard surface, will give passengers no trouble. As in the Ford, driver and passengers are aware of the surface without being bothered by it.

The body leans more than before, and passengers will be pitched about very slightly more than in previous models.

Is the Engine Compartment Cluttered?

It's one of the cleanest we've seen, even allowing for the power equipment not present on the test car. An enormous space in front of the radiator is useless, but you can get around the compact V8 with refreshing ease. A giant air cleaner assembly has to be removed for any serious work. Plugs are inaccessible.

What's Different About a Chevrolet?

You'll like a firmly put-together air, characteristic of its Fisher bodies for years past and of its chassis since 1955. Along with the V8's smoothness, the high quality of interior trim, the softer ride and the use of various components present in bigger GM cars, this can almost make you think you're in a higher price bracket. Specific features worthy of engineering respect and exclusive to Chevrolet in its field are the light-weight engine and the Turboglide, which we heartily recommend if a Chevy is your choice and it's optional on the model you want. Unsurpassed smoothness and accelerating power combine with the new HR (hill retarder) range to make as *satisfying* a transmission as any automatic we've driven. In our brief test on the GM Proving Ground at Milford, Mich., it slowed us down on steep grades as though with a giant hand, which it should since this is its only function. It gives no advantage in acceleration (not that one is needed!) and so makes Turboglide just about as completely automatic as it can get until the day when it can see a hill ahead and decide itself to shift to the hill retarder.

Chevrolet continues the GM keyless locking system. A Chevy driver has two blessed conveniences missing from the Ford and Plymouth: a centered glove compartment, and complete absence of distortion in the wrap-around windshield. We regard both as minimal requirements in a modern car. Nor are they conveniences alone; both are aids to safety and all manufacturers should adopt them permanently in 1958, even over the wails of their stylists.

You get the most accurate speedometer in any U.S. car.

The new low-set tail lights, smaller than most, do not give adequate protection against rear-end collisions.

Will It Last a Long Time?

A car that is *not* all new is likely to be a better bet for the long-term owner than one that still has some wrinkles to be ironed out during the first model year. A poorly hung rear door whose window was extremely tough to roll down, uneven paint on the dash molding, and badly fitting brightwork on the dash itself marred the looks of the test car. Check these points (which should be improved later in the year) along with quality of exterior paint and any rear-axle hum in the particular Chevy that meets your specifications.

Access to the driver's seat is good, but the seat doesn't adjust far enough to the rear. Tall people will bump their knees on the steering wheel.

LEG CONTORTIONS are required in entering the rear seat, but there is little real difficulty since the high roof line doesn't interfere as it does in the Ford and Plymouth, where a bumped head is the rule.

CHEVY TRUNK can only be unlatched with the key. Lid lifts to reveal entirely adequate compartment, good spare location. Bumper-type jack fits behind spare, didn't work in tests performed in trying to replace flat tire.

P E R F O R M A N C E

'57

(270-bhp engine)

ACCELERATION From Standing Start
0-45 mph 6.75   0-60 mph 9.9
Quarter-mile 17.5 and 77.5 mph
Passing Speeds
30-50 mph 3.55   45-60 mph 2.9
50-80 mph 9.9

FUEL CONSUMPTION Used Mobilgas Special
Steady Speeds
16.75 mpg @ 30   14.8 mpg @ 45
13.1 mpg @ 60   12.2 mpg @ 75
Stop-and-Go Driving
13.6 mpg tank average for 136 miles
Highway Driving
15.0 mpg tank average for 312 miles

OIL CONSUMPTION One quart added in 974 miles

SPEEDOMETER ERROR Read 30 at true 30, 45 at 45, 51 at
50, 60 at 60, 76.5 at 75, 81.5 at 80

'56

(205-bhp engine)

ACCELERATION From Standing Start
0-30 mph 4.2   0-60 mph 10.7
Quarter-mile 18.3 and 76 mph
Passing Speeds
30-50 mph 3.9   50-80 mph 12.0

FUEL CONSUMPTION Used Mobilgas Special
Steady Speeds
20.8 mpg @ 30   19.4 mpg @ 45
16.6 mpg @ 60   13.6 mpg @ 75
Stop-and-Go Driving
14.2 mpg tank average for 800
miles

SPEEDOMETER ERROR Read 31 at true 30, 47 at 45, 63
at 60, and 78 at 75

SPECIAL 1957 SHOW ISSUE !

CHEVROLET'S STRONG POINTS FOR 1957 ARE QUALITY AND PERFORMANCE. THIS IS ONE OF TWO BEL AIR TEST CARS.

Chevrolet Road Test

WHAT does Chevrolet have for 1957? Plenty, of course. Never before has it had so much to offer. And—as a matter of fact—never has it needed it more.

Last year Chevy had things pretty much its own way. The competition was tough, but the products of Flint were hard to beat in any department. But now the picture has changed —and considerably would be a weak word to describe it.

All of Chevrolet's major rivals have gone all-out—developed smart, fresh body designs backed up by solid and completely new chassis engineering. It's going to take a better than good car to hold the line against them.

Nonetheless, it's been no accident that Chevy's has been top dog for a couple of decades. It is put out by men who know how to build good cars, cars that people want.

The dramatic announcement of fuel injection can be disregarded, for all practical purposes, where the average driver is concerned. The unit will be in limited supply; furthermore, the extra cost of the setup makes carburetion still look pretty appealing. But there are other cards in the deck than this and a road test indicates just about how Chevrolet intends to play them.

Two cars were used for this test report. The one in which the most miles were covered was a Bel Air four-door sedan, equipped with the 185-hp engine, Powerglide transmission, power brakes and steering. The second test car, used primarily for additional performance figures, was virtually identical, except for the engine which was the optional Corvette V-8 of 283 cubic inches that develops 270 hp at 6000 rpm—with two four-barrel carburetors, eight throats or one for each cylinder!

Since it was obvious long in advance that Chevrolet's rivals would have their biggest guns in styling, the top brass at GM OK'd many more extra millions of dollars for extensive body surgery on the two-year-old shell. The results are a Buickish grille and a dash of Cadillac at the finned rear. There are many other alterations, of course, and the overall effect is undeniably good, the car looks better than ever. But is it

good enough? Good question. Fashions are changing fast.

If its styling is not up to par for 1957, Chevrolet has something else to offer in eye appeal. Something that, regrettably, is almost too exclusive. That item is quality. It can't be missed, even in the most casual inspection. And Chevy hits a new high in its price class in this respect, in fact surpasses many higher-priced makes.

The materials are sound and substantial, with precision finish abundantly evident. On the test cars, everything was as tight and solid as could be expected in a mass-crafted car, well matched, durable.

This quality, coupled with its other features, could make Chevrolet the most *car* per dollar that any buyer could find anywhere!

Performance has been almost synonymous with Chevrolet ever since the V-8 version bowed in 1955. It still is.

Take the test car with the lower power rating, as a case in point. Although it boasts "only" 185 hp, it belted out acceleration times that power-kitted versions of rival makes would find it hard to melt. From the bottom to the top of the clock, the marks achieved were just fractions of a second off what models with 50 more hp struggle to record.

From 0-60 mph, for instance, the 185-hp Chevy registered a flat 11 seconds—quick enough for any road or traffic. Nor did it waste any of its energy burning rubber (good weight distribution helps).

On the other hand, the more potent 270-hp model, with higher compression and two four-barrels, charged from a standing start to 60 mph in 8.2 seconds. It should be noted that this is with the Corvette V-8 hooked to a Powerglide unit. Match it with the new three-speed box or a stick shift—and stand back!

Fuel consumption of the compact V-8, mounted inside one of Detroit's tidiest engine compartments, is a hair above average. The 185-hp edition yielded 15.4 for combined city and open highway driving.

BUMPER EXHAUSTS are simulated, real outlet is conventional pipe barely seen underneath the car. Gas cap is concealed behind hinged flap at rear of fin. Chevrolet trim fit is exceptionally good.

EMPTY SPACE, almost big enough to crawl into, is between the radiator and grille. Chevy hood is virtually unbeatable when it comes to easy latching and lifting. Engine area is comparatively uncluttered.

The 1957 Chevrolet is properly obedient on normal roads, actually handles and feels like one of its heavier GM brothers. On a winding route or around sharp corners, however, it leans, causes too much discomfort among its passengers. As a matter of fact, it is one of those rare cases in which a car falls below the standard it set in the previous year.

From behind the wheel, the seating position is good only by pre-1957 standards. The seats are high and erect, the steering rim has not yet been brought down to the sports-type angle or size for maximum ease. On the other hand, the interior is more spacious, while the bench seat will contain three persons abreast without undue interference from the transmission-driveline hump. Exit and entry are superior to some, but not all, of the lower cars which have sacrificed door area room on the altar of looks, especially where corner posts protrude.

The dash layout has been improved and rearranged. Instruments now recessed in attractive bright-metal casings hold reflections to a minimum, yet allow good visibility. Distortion in the wrap windshield has been whipped. And the centrally located glove box is a bonus feature.

The Chevrolet speedometer is worthy of special notice. On the average it is dead accurate; on the test car checked it held true up to 60 mph, where it turned out to be just one mph fast—actual speed being 59 mph.

There are other new touches on the 1957 Chevy. Twin hood ornaments (called "windsplits") run counter to the current clean-hood trend; the gas cap is now concealed behind a flap at the rear of the lefthand tail fin; and the fresh air intakes for interior ventilating have been moved from the cowl to a position under the headlight hoods.

These then are the highlights of the 1957 Chevrolet. How does it all add up?

The car has been extensively restyled to bring it up to date, but it's still short of the "new look." On the other side, it has outstanding quality and exceptional performance—and these are long-term values. Maybe the compromise is the happy combination buyers want. If so, Chevrolet will prove it this year.

GOOD DASH layout includes simple arrangement of instruments, centrally located glove box, easy-to-reach controls. The speedometer is almost dead accurate. Steering wheel position could be improved.

CHEVROLET TEST DATA

Test Cars: Bel Air series four-door sedans
Basic Price: $2230
Dimensions: Length 200 inches, width 74, height 60.5, tread 58, wheelbase 115
Dry Weight: 3390 lbs
Transmissions: PowerGlide torque converter
Speedometer Corrections: Indicated 30, 45 and 60 mph are actual 30, 45 and 61, respectively

ENGINE WITHOUT POWER KIT

Displacement: 283 cubic inches
Compression Ratio: 8.5-to-1
Horsepower: 185 @ 4600 rpm
Torque: 275 lbs/ft @ 2400 rpm
Carburetor: Two-barrel
Acceleration: 0-30 mph 3.7 seconds, 0-45 mph 6.4 and 0-60 mph 11 seconds
Gas Mileage: 15 mpg average

OPTIONAL CORVETTE V-8

Displacement: 283 cubic inches
Compression Ratio: 9.5-to-1
Horsepower: 270 @ 6000 rpm
Torque: 285 lbs/ft @ 4200 rpm
Carburetor: two four-barrels
Acceleration: 0-30 mph 3.3 seconds, 0-45 mph 5.6 and 0-60 mph 8.2 seconds

CHEVROLET

By JAMES WHIPPLE

CHEVROLET offers the buyer of a low-priced car of 1957 an almost bewildering array of engines, power options and transmission combinations ranging from the familiar and reliable overhead valve six (now upped to 140 bhp) to a fabulously powerful V8 engine of 283 cubic inches displacement developing 283 bhp with the aid of a new fuel injection system.

Other engine options are a 265 cubic-inch V8 of 162 bhp and versions of the 283 cubic-inch engine developing 185, 220, 245, 250, 270 and, of course, 283 horsepower. The variations in the 283 cubic-inch engine's output are the result of combinations of power boosting modifications such as dual exhausts, four-barrel carburetors, high-performance valve timing and the like.

Transmission choices include standard synchromesh, synchromesh with overdrive, Powerglide and new Turboglide automatics. Any of these power transmission options may be had with any engine except that Turboglide transmissions are only available on the 283 cubic-inch-displacement engines. There are a total of 22 engine and drive combinations available.

Much of the buyer's choice will be determined by the cost of the optional high performance engines and the type of transmission he prefers.

We feel that the 220 bhp "Super Turbo Fire 283" engine with either manual or automatic transmissions will deliver all the power that 95 out of 100 drivers can use efficiently.

With the higher-powered engines of 250 and 270 horsepower the Chevy definitely becomes a "hot" automobile with a potential for reaching speeds in excess of 100 miles per hour in a very short space of time. The performance of these "hottest" engines (over the 220 bhp engine) will be mostly in speed ranges well over legal limits.

These hot engines will enable Chevy owners to jump out into the left lane, pass and hop back into the right lane in less time than ever before and will also require (in such high-speed maneuvers) quicker reactions and better judgment than ever before. We feel that the man who orders a 283-bhp Chevy should be prepared to handle a car that offers one horsepower for each 13 pounds of total weight, and can reach 60 miles per hour in about 9 seconds from a standstill.

Beneath the excitement created by the sensational (for light, low-priced cars) horsepower, the '57 Chevy is an excellent automobile with a tested, stable design and a very satisfactory level of quality and workmanship.

Bel Air convertible shows longer look
achieved by fins, single horizontal strip
and thrusting headlight cowl.

ENGINES	SIX	TURBO-FIRE "265" V-8	SUPER TURBO-FIRE "283" V-8
Bore and stroke	3⁹⁄₁₆ in. x 3¹⁵⁄₁₆ in.	3.75 in. x 3 in.	3.87 in. x 3 in.
Displacement	235.5 cu. in.	265 cu. in.	283 cu. in.
Compression ratio	8.0:1	8.0:1	8.5:1
Max. brake horsepower	140	162	220
Max. Torque	210 @ 2400		
DIMENSIONS			
Wheelbase	115 in.		
Overall length	200 in.		
Overall width	73.9 in.		
Overall height	60.5 in.		
TRANSMISSIONS	Standard synchromesh, Overdrive, Powerglide, Turboglide		
PRICE RANGE	(FOB Detroit) $1,680 (Six) to $2,354 (V-8)		

Lowered silhouettes are a 1957 feature. Actually, Chevrolet has made little change in its exterior design, except for trim. The rear fender fins are a '57 innovation.

Most of the changes made in the '57 Chevy are refinements of a solid and successful car (1957 is the third model-year for the basic body shell and chassis of the car).

Beside the visible styling changes of grille, headlight area, rear fender panels (bigger fins), taillights, bumpers, and hood ornamentation, Chevy has a new, lower cowl line and hood which increases windshield area and makes a slight improvement in forward vision.

Heating and ventilation air intakes have been incorporated in the hoods of the headlights instead of in the cowl for reasons best known to Chevrolet's engineers. (The other two members of the big three have just switched to cowl air intakes.)

Interior body dimensions are the same as they were last year. The overall height of the car is also unchanged and now is four inches (more or less) higher than the other members of the big three. Prospective buyers, especially tall ones, will notice the difference when "trying on" the low-priced three in rapid succession. The higher (old fashioned?) Chevy is easier to get in and out of especially in the case of back-seat passengers entering and leaving two-door models.

The seating positions (both front and rear) of the Chevy are higher than some of the completely re-designed '57's and the transmission hump and driveshaft tunnel are less noticeable in the passenger compartment.

For some people, the higher seating position and easier entry and exit could be the deciding factor in a choice between Chevy and one of the ultra-low completely re-designed '57s.

The question is not that these lower cars will be fundamentally less comfortable for everyone, as their riding comfort is excellent, in some cases actually softer than Chevy's, but that the more erect seating of the Chevy may suit some people's posture comfort better than the easy-chair seating position of the low, low cars.

We can't attempt to tell you which will be more comfortable for you; what we can do, however, is advise that you try both types for yourself.

Chevy interiors are, as usual, comfortable and well made even if a bit over-decorated on the luxury Bel Air models. The new instrument cluster, which is mounted in a turret high on the panel and just below windshield eye-level, is excellent. The black dials have glowing green (black-

lighted) numerals that show up clearly at night.

The Chevy's ride is well-controlled and happily free from sway and pitching, but it is not as soft and vibration-free as some of the other cars in the same price class. Once again, Chevy has made an engineering choice in favor of comfort via control and a more solid grip on the road as against the soft, marshmallow suspension action that blots up all of the harsh qualities that stem from rough surfaces but leaves the passengers bobbing, rolling, weaving and mushing on the turns.

The stability and ruggedness of the Chevy's body structure is very good as it has been in the past. Even the four door hardtop has very little shake, and that's a notoriously "loose" body type.

Steering is good as always with the Saginaw re-circulating ball gear set-up which reduces steering effort to a minimum. Most owners will not feel the need of power steering, although the woman driver whose motoring is done in congested traffic may find it helpful.

Even with power steering, some owners will find, if they've purchased a Chevy with one of the high-performance engines, that the steering is not "quick" enough for high-speed driving on all but the most perfect road surfaces.

Also in this connection we suggest that Chevy's power brakes be optioned with the more powerful engines. These power brakes have an excellent "feel" and permit perfect control. Adjustment of Chevy's brakes during the break-in period is still a problem until the linings are "bedded in."

As in the past, Chevrolet's firmer-than-average suspension provides good roadability on indifferent surfaces and winding high-crowned roads. However it would be well for buyers of the "hot" engined Chevy to remember that the Chevy is a "family" car and cannot provide the high-speed road-holding ability of a sports car chassis such as the Corvette's.

SUMMING UP: Chevrolet is a well-built car with a roomy, comfortable body on a solid chassis offering a good compromise between maximum roadability and an ultra-soft ride. An unusually wide choice of power plants and transmissions offers buyers the option of economy (six cylinder engine) driving ease (Turboglide transmission and power steering) and performance (250, 270 and 283 bhp engines). ●

Dashboard has '57 "new look." Instruments
are concentrated under a deep hood
super-imposed on the dash panel crown.
Gauges are full face with red indicators.

CHEVROLET
is the car
for you

If . . . You want one of the most
spectacular performers
available in any price class.

If . . . You prefer slightly conservative
styling emphasizing massive
lines and solid trim.

If . . . You find that a body with
higher roof line and seating
position is easier to enter
or sit in.

If . . . You want a car with an
excellent combination of
comfortable ride and a stable,
roadable chassis.

CHEVROLET CHECK LIST

☑ ☑
☑ ☑ ☑   **5 CHECKS MEANS TOP RATING**

PERFORMANCE	Chevrolet with optional high-performance engines and fuel injection offers the greatest performance potential in its price field.	✔ ✔ ✔ ✔ ✔
STYLING	As in the past, Chevy styling is on the massive and conservative side rather than of the "jet plane" type of design. Overall effect of the '57 Chevy's longer look and more flowing side chrome trim will be liked by most people.	✔ ✔ ✔ ✔
RIDING COMFORT	As in years past, Chevrolet strikes a balance between a ride that's cushion soft and undulating with one that is very tautly sprung in the interests of maximum stability.	✔ ✔ ✔ ✔
INTERIOR DESIGN	This year Chevy offers an alternative to the lower seating positions and "stoop-to-enter" design of some of the other cars in its price field. Seat cushions are properly firm and vision is good.	✔ ✔ ✔ ✔
ROADABILITY	Although still better than average, Chevy is no longer tops in its class in this respect. As in the past Chevy's road holding ability will be very satisfactory for most drivers.	✔ ✔ ✔ ✔
EASE OF CONTROL	New Turboglide transmission offers perhaps the smoothest power flow at all speeds of any car. Average drivers will appreciate power assist for Chevy's higher than average brake pedal pressures. Steering gear is one of the best in the industry.	✔ ✔ ✔ ✔
ECONOMY	The combination of Powerglide transmission and the Chevy V8 is not the most frugal combination in the low-priced class. The six-cylinder engine with overdrive transmission is the ecomony-minded buyer's best bet. (We have not yet tested the fuel consumption characteristics of either the fuel injection engine of Turboglide transmission.)	✔ ✔ ✔
SERVICEABILITY	Chevy is one of the most accessible and well laid-out chassis in its class. For '57 the battery has been made even easier to service.	✔ ✔ ✔ ✔
WORKMANSHIP	Generally better than average. Paint finish of panels and chrome-plate is very good. Occasional flaws show up in the fit of interior trim and upholstery.	✔ ✔ ✔ ✔
VALUE PER DOLLAR	Although Chevrolet has the lowest depreciation of any car in its field and has a good record of durability, the '57 model is a face-lift competing with some entirely "new" cars, and the depreciation could be a bit higher for this model.	✔ ✔ ✔ ✔

CHEVROLET OVERALL RATING . . . 4.0 CHECKS

Johnnie Tolan TESTS the '57 CHEVROLET

On a road-racing course and through rush-hour traffic, Johnnie Tolan puts the '57 Chevrolet through its paces, comes away pleased with looks and handling.

FOR a professional racing driver, trying out a new model car is second only to actual racing for kicks. So when SPEED AGE asked me to track-test the '57 Chevrolet, I was delighted with the assignment.

I was still delighted when it was over.

For the most part, I was impressed with the new Chevy—liked its looks as well as its performance, although it is not without faults.

Since styling has been one of the major changes this year, to the eye at least, we might begin there and see what Chevrolet has to offer for '57.

As car enthusiasts are aware by now, General Motors has not gone quite as far as the competition with radical design changes. But if GM's styling isn't as spectacular as the high swept fins and bold lines on other new models, it has plenty of eye appeal. I thought this was especially true of the Chevy.

This year's Chevrolet is not completely a different car from last year's —although there have been major face-lifting changes. The changes appear more natural—maybe even conservative—than in most '57 cars.

One of the most prominent additions is a pair of wide spread hood ornaments, which extend from two "bumps" or creases running the length of the hood. These eye catchers, which Chevrolet calls "windsplits," are apparently intended to break up the flat, empty effect the hood would have otherwise.

I didn't find them unappealing but I

No one knows as much about Detroit's production cars as the nation's top stock car race drivers. Day after day, on all kinds of road surfaces and under all conditions, these men put stock cars through grueling trials and tests in competition with one another.

In view of these facts, SPEED AGE has arranged for a series of tests of all Detroit cars by some of the nation's leading race drivers. We feel it will assure our readers of the inside story on performance and handling as interpreted by the men best qualified to judge.

This month Johnnie Tolan brings you his EXPERT TESTS of the 1957 Chevrolet and Oldsmobile.

SPECIFICATIONS:
1956 CHEVROLET
BEL AIR
4-DOOR SEDAN

ENGINE:

MODEL	SUPER TURBO-FIRE V-8
CYLINDERS	V-8
VALVES	OHV
DISPLACEMENT	283 CU. IN.
BORE	3.87 INCHES
STROKE	3.00 INCHES
COMPRESSION RATIO	9.5:1
MAXIMUM BHP	185 @ 4600 RPM
MAXIMUM TORQUE	275 @ 2400 RPM
CARBURETOR	SINGLE QUAD

DIMENSIONS:

WHEELBASE	115 INCHES
TREAD: FRONT	58.0 INCHES
REAR	58.8 INCHES
LENGTH OVERALL	200 INCHES
WIDTH OVERALL	73.9 INCHES
HEIGHT OVERALL	60.5 INCHES

GEARING:

REAR AXLE	3.36:1
TRANSMISSION (POWERGLIDE)	1.82:1 LOW
	1.00:1 DRIVE
	1.82:1 REVERSE

PERFORMANCE:

TOP SPEED	111.3 MPH
0-60 MPH	9.3 SECONDS
0-50 MPH	7.0 SECONDS
0-40 MPH	5.2 SECONDS
0-30 MPH	4.0 SECONDS

Innovations on this 1957 Chevrolet Bel Air Sport Sedan include optional fuel injection and 14-inch wheels. A choice of five engines and four transmissions is offered, plus power steering and power brakes.

imagine it will take a little time to get used to them. It's something like a race car that usually has a hood unbroken by a bump of any kind, until lately. Now many of them have a protruding bump, and if the race car runs good, that bump gets better looking all the time!

Chevrolet designers did a neat job on a brand-new grille and front bumper this year. The lines are simple, without a lot of gingerbread but still decorative and practical. The same goes for the rear bumper, which gives the appearance of having dual exhausts moulded into it. The rear part of the car, with its prominent but conservative fender fins, struck me fine. The

gasoline filler neck is concealed in the left rear fin where it is accessible but neatly hidden when not in use.

The taillights probably would have been more practical and less confusing to the guy driving behind, if they had been located higher on the rear fender fins. They're set pretty low and could be distracting to other drivers at night. But I like the lights themselves because they are not those big beacons that some cars have, scaring a guy into thinking he's just run onto a police car.

One more thing on body style before we get inside. Just back of the headlights, on the side of each fender, are three louver-like ornaments. I noticed

them because on our test car, they had been put on crooked. My first impression was that they were something thrown on in a last minute decision. But looking at them and the body lines more carefully, I could see that they serve a definite purpose in breaking up a look of too much empty space along the fenders.

Now we climb inside. This year's Chevrolet has one of the finest interiors I've seen in a low priced car. The fabrics used on the seats and doors are rich looking, although the headliner looked a bit cheap by comparison. The dash board and instrument panel of our Bel Air four-door sedan test car were real eye catchers. The instru-

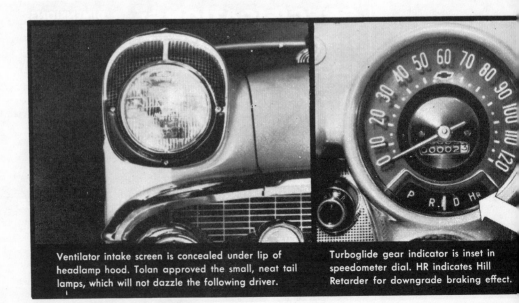

Ventilator intake screen is concealed under lip of headlamp hood. Tolan approved the small, neat tail lamps, which will not dazzle the following driver.

Turboglide gear indicator is inset in speedometer dial. HR indicates Hill Retarder for downgrade braking effect.

Concealed but easily accessible gasoline filler neck is an extra feature Tolan approved.

Driver Tolan has reservations on carburetor air cleaner intake. Here he points out opening he thinks too small for efficiency.

Johnnie liked effect of the fender ornaments, even though one on the test car was out of line.

ment panel is set directly in front of the driver where every instrument can be seen clearly. Even the turn indicators are mounted in the same group where they can be seen.

There is plenty of head and leg room throughout, and I was pleased particularly with the sitting position of both the front and rear cushions. They were wide enough so that the edge of the seat struck the back of my legs, just above the knees. I've driven cars, especially race cars, where the seat was narrow and offered too little support for a comfortable sitting position. As a result I get fatigued more quickly.

Another interior feature I liked was

the location of the ignition switch. How many times have you gotten into a car with the key in your right hand—if you're right handed like most people —and discovered the ignition switch is on the left. So you fumble to find it. It may sound silly, but it can be a nuisance. The Chevy, however, has the switch located just to the right of the instrument panel where it's most convenient.

Now, the power plant which, these days, is a major issue with horse-power minded motorists. Five engines are available this year, including the Corvette V-8, a 283 cubic inch job with twin four-barrel carburetion. There are two versions of this power plant, one

with the four-barrel carburetion and one with fuel injection.

Fuel injection was put to practical use at the Indianapolis Motor Speedway, as far back as 1948. But until recently its use was limited almost entirely to the 500-mile race, which did a great deal to develop and improve the device. Now it's being put to use in passenger cars and probably will become standard in years to come.

The Super Turbo-Fire V-8 engine, also with 283 inches and 9.5 to one compression is available with single four-barrel carburetion, and then there is the Turbo-Fire V-8 with two-barrel carburetion, 8.5 to one compression

Continued on page **100**

Restyled front end of the '57 is handsome, neat and uncluttered, although somewhat reminiscent of last year's Buick styling.

Johnnie Tolan drives the Bel Air sedan he tested on the new road-racing course at Paramount Ranch near Agura, California. But Tolan considers the drive home through downtown L.A. and Freeway traffic was the most telling part of the test.

1955

1956

1957

'55 to '57... The Good Old Years

An intimate look at what makes the mid-Fifties nifties the sought-after classics they remain today.

By Jay Storer

Back in late 1954, Chevrolet introduced the car that changed their history—the 1955 model with optional V-8 engine, Chevy's first V-8 since 1918. More new and impressive engineering features were introduced on the '55 model than on any other Chevy, past or present. It was a whole new ball game starting with this car that almost immediately put Chevrolet into, and on top of, the performance car field and also signaled the beginning of a slow death for the flathead Ford after a 20-yr. reign as King of Engines.

What made this new Chevy so popular, then and now? In the public's eye, probably the most important feature was the 265-cu.-in. V-8, the granddaddy of the 283-307-327-350-400 engines that were to follow. Almost a million of those '55 265's were sold, proving that its successful design gave people what they wanted. With 8.1:1 compression, the 265 could be purchased at the standard level of 162 hp with 2-bbl. carb, or in the "hot" version at 180 hp with a 4-bbl. and dual exhausts. At the time, these engines were hotter than any of the 6's Chevy had ever offered, even the 150-hp Corvette "Blue Flame" 6.

The '55 also represented a completely new vehicle in styling and engineering. Almost everything was a departure from 1954, starting with the body, which was more like a square than a pear, with its new wraparound windshield offered much more total glass area for visibility. Most of the outdated chassis design was eliminated, too. This new car had modern ball joint front suspension rather than kingpins, an open driveshaft and Hotchkiss rear end rather than torque tube drive, new ball/race steering gear, and a new, integral front crossmember rather than the old heavy bolt-on type. Features such as these reduced the chassis weight, and at the same time actually increased its strength. Other new features introduced in 1955 include overhead "swinging" pedals, tubeless tires for a better ride and more safety, a 12-volt electrical system, and a "Touch-Down" overdrive. In fact, the car represented such a departure in engineering that it was chosen for the pace car at the 1955 running of the Indy 500. (The best speeds for the race cars were bordering on 130 mph at that time.)

The next year saw improvements and refinements in styling and engineering, but the basic car was the same. The '55 had proven the package. The '56 styling was changed in the front and rear, it had different side trim, and the gas tank filler neck was now concealed behind the left taillight housing instead of on the left rear fender. In fact, on the bottom-of-the-line model 150 Chevys, 1956 was the first year that *any* chrome trim was used.

Other than the new styling, most of the other changes that year were in the option availability. Directional signals, previously an option, were made standard equipment for the first time. New 4-door "sport sedans" and 9-passenger station wagons were introduced, bringing the total line-up to 19 models of Chevys. It's interesting to note now that seat belts *and* shoulder harnesses were both offered as options back in '56. In the engineering department, the starter motors now had a rubber cover over the solenoid plunger, and horsepower ratings were upped on all engines. The standard 6 was raised to 140 hp at 8:1 compression and was the only 6 offered. However, the 265 V-8 now came in three configurations: standard at 162 hp for standard shift cars, 170 hp for the Powerglides, and a special 205 hp "power pack" model with 4-bbl., dual exhausts and 9.25:1 compression. One of the few areas in the original 265 where something was lacking was the oil filter, so a new "full-flow" oil filter became an option in '56. This was a replaceable cartridge mounted in a steel canister under the left rear part of the block, a feature that later became standard, up until 1968 when Chevy started using spin-on filters.

The next year brought even more changes, and changes that put Chevrolet solidly on top of the performance car field. Again the basic shape of the body was the same, but the front end was new and the rear fenders extended into fins, as was the trend in the late '50's. The 1957 Chevy was almost as much a new vehicle in engineering as the '55 had been. The major new features included a new Turboglide automatic transmission option, a new engine, the destined-to-be-famous 283, and a top-of-the-line engine option featuring fuel injection.

1955

1956

1957

'55 to '57...

Of interest perhaps only to students of the '55-'57 Chevy, the glass area was again increased, the battery was moved from the firewall to up front by the radiator, a "unitized" starter motor was used, and the tires and wheels were switched from 6.70x15 to 7.50x14 "low pressure" (22 lbs.).

In 1957, performance options were where it was happening. Chevrolet was figuratively and literally racing Ford for the prestige of being the top car on the high banks of the big NASCAR races. Chevy had its 283-hp Rochester fuel injection model, while Ford came up with their Mc-Culloch-blown 312's to compete with that, and the Oldsmobiles were running the J-2 tri-power engine! All of these cars were also jousting hotly in the superstock ranks at the drags. But as far as the range and variety of performance options go, Chevy had all the other manufacturers beat, and automotive history has proven that they had the best basic engine design to work from. The small-block Chevy has always put out more rpm's, torque and horsepower for its size than it had any right to, and the '57

Chevy fuel injection model was the first domestic production engine to boast of the magic and elusive volumetric efficiency of 1 hp/cu. in. A lightweight engine, its oversquare design (the bore is bigger than the stroke), good breathing characteristics, and a lightweight valve train capable of high rpm's all contributed to the V-8's success in the racing world.

A total of eight engine horsepower models were offered in 1957, the majority of them in the high-performance category. The basic Stovebolt 6 was still offered at 140 hp with 8:1 compression and a 1-bbl. carburetor, but enthusiasm for the V-8 heavily overshadowed it. The 265 V-8 was still available with a 2-bbl. carb, 8:1 compression and 162 hp (offered only with standard transmission in '57), but 1957 was the last year the 265 was produced. After that it was 283 all the way, that engine becoming the Chevy mainstay for the next decade. The two basic passenger car 283's were the Turbo-Fire with 2-bbl., 8.5:1 C.R., and 185 hp, and the "Super" Turbo-Fire which had 9.5:1 C.R., with 4-bbl. and dual exhausts, and put out 220 hp. The

four other engines were so-called "Corvette 283" options, although they were available in the passenger cars too. All of these had dual exhausts and three had 9.5:1 C.R.; their horsepower ratings being 245 with dual quads, 250 with fuel injection, 270 with dual quads and competition cam, and the big daddy, of course, was the 283 which had the Duntov cam, fuel injection and 10.5:1 C.R.

One of the interesting chassis and driveline features in '57 was the semi-centrifugal clutch that was standard on the 4-bbl. and hotter engines. This was a standard 3-finger clutch design, but it also had three floating rollers or weights spaced around the clutch cover that would, under centrifugal force, add pressure due to a rolling wedge action at higher rpms. This allowed a higher effective clutch pressure without affecting pedal effort under normal conditions. Other innovations for 1957 included the introduction of the famous "window" distributor, which permitted easy point dwell adjustments with the distributor still on the engine and the engine running. The new engines featured another now familiar part, the "ram's horn" exhaust manifolds

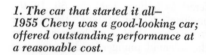

1. The car that started it all— 1955 Chevy was a good-looking car; offered outstanding performance at a reasonable cost.

2. The 1955 front end represented a radical change from previous years with ball joints, not kingpins.

3. The basic design of that first 265 V-8 is still being used today in all the later small-blocks.

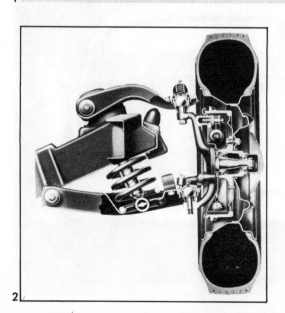

which offered better breathing than most stock Detroit types. The full-flow oil filter was made standard on both the dual quad and fuel injection engines.

Chevrolet engineers had reworked the chassis to compensate for the power of all these extra engine options, and wound up with a winning combination for street, drags and oval track racing! In fact, although it wasn't too well known outside the racing fraternity, Chevy published a small booklet in '57 that, without fanfare or flash, told you exactly how to build a race car from a standard 150 or 210 2-door sedan. The parts and numbers were listed and explained, and specs, power figures, special heavy-duty options, tuning tips and troubleshooting data were all made available within the pages of this seemingly innocent booklet. This reduced the problems of making a racing stock car to a simple matter of walking into the dealer's parts counter with checkbook and this competition guide in hand. Well, almost that simple.

It was at this point, with all the factories getting heavily into the

4

5

4. The '55 station wagon was one of the first wagons that didn't look "fat" or bulging.

5. Two-tone paint was a hot item in the mid-'50's, and the styling of the Bel Air lent itself to a good looking treatment.

6. The first really hot passenger car engine option was the dual-quad, solid lifter, 225-hp "Corvette". It turned in high 15's at 90+ mph. High-lift cam might still be a good bet for a street 265 or 283 engine.

7. The 150 model was cheapest in the Chevy line. Being the lightest, it's the best starting point for a race car. The '56 was first of the 150's to have any chrome trim.

8. Long the favorite of the racing crowd for its weight transfer, the 150 sedan delivery is fast becoming a collector's item for the street crowd, like the Nomad wagon; '56 had beautifully simple side trim.

8

'55 to '57...

NASCAR and drag racing picture, that the Automobile Manufacturers Association decided things had gone too far and stepped in. The AMA got GM and the other manufacturers to sign a ban on factory participation or active support of racing. What this meant for Chevrolet was only that they continued to produce good engines and a host of racing parts (usually listed in the parts books as "truck," "heavy-duty," or "marine" parts), but they just didn't show any ostensible interest in racing. The fuel injection, though never again offered on passenger cars, was retained as an option for the Corvette until 1965, at which time the system was dropped because it usually ran too rich to pass smog tests and because there weren't enough mechanics trained to work on it.

So it was with these three mid-'50's cars, the '55-'57, that Chevrolet took hold of the performance world, and established a reputation for equipment that adapted easily to racing. It's easy to see how these cars were the hot rodders' favorites then, but they are as popular today, if not more so, than when they rolled off the assembly line some 15 yrs. ago. Rodders recognized the efficiency of the Chevy V-8 right from the start, and almost right after the cars were introduced, they were being raced and modified. So the California speed equipment manufacturers who knew a good thing when they saw it, jumped in hands and feet and began turning out rafts of bolt-on parts for the stovebolt bent-8. Because the follow-up engines to the 265, the 283-307-327-350-400, were all the same basic size with many parts interchangeable, there is probably more Chevy speed equipment extant today than for any other engine ever built! This has a good deal to do with the tremendous popularity that these cars still retain. Their light but strong chassis were easily reworked for racing and handling, the engine compartments were big enough to make working on the engines comparatively easy, every kind of speed or custom part designed was available, and the cars were cheap, easy to work on, and reliable enough, even when modified, to make them ideally suited for dual-purpose cars with hot street performance and the flexibility for basic transportation.

A gaggle of these cars are still on the street; you see them everywhere, with rumbling idles and packed-up suspensions, and you can still buy one at a used car lot for a reasonable price, although some dealers are getting wise to how popular these cars are and they charge quite a bit more than "book" value. With a new paint job, some upholstery work, mag wheels, and maybe some new chrome for the bumpers, these cars are still good looking transportation. The interior and trunk are roomy enough to carry all your friends, spare parts and tools. So now that you know what makes these cars so popular, don't just rush out to buy one; hang in with us and we'll tell you how the '55-'57 can be set up for street 'n' strip.

REWORKING THE CHASSIS

Unfortunately, judging by the cars we see every day on the highway and at the hamburger stands, when many guys think of "setting up" the chassis on an early Chevy, their only concern is how to get it way up in the air. The bad part about this is that the modifications they usually make to jack the car up are highly detrimental to handling and safety. This

1

2

3

4

whole business of jacking up cars front and rear, after a long street tradition of "raking" the car to the front or back, was started around 1964, when funny cars were just starting and many of the gassers and modified production cars were experimenting with a high center of gravity for more weight transfer. The idea caught on with the street crowd because they wanted a gutsy, drag racing look on their own cars. But while drag racing has long since abandoned the high-altitude approach, we still see horrendous examples on the street.

Naturally, there is a right and a wrong way to do anything. One of the most common methods used to jack up the mid-'50's Chevy is the use of ultra-long rear spring shackles. These are cheap at $8-$12 and they're sold in every speed shop, parts house and department store in the country, but most of them are too long. They offer several sets of holes in them for various heights, and we wouldn't recommend using any holes beyond the set at the top. In fact, for any *street* machine—Ford, Plymouth or Chevy — we don't think it's a good idea to alter the stock height by more than 2 ins. up or down. With the car too high, it will handle badly in freeway crosswinds and will lean over on corners, and the really long shackles put too much leverage on the spring eye. With your 3200-lb. Chevy swaying in the breeze atop

5

6

1. The 1957 Bel Air Sport Coupe is to many Chevy fans the best-looking Chevy ever built. We find it hard to disagree with them!

2. The famous 283 was introduced in '57 amid a host of engineering changes, including battery up by the radiator, ram's horn exhaust manifolds and "window" distributor.

3. This unique air cleaner setup was part of the dual-quad option if it was ordered in a passenger car. On the 283, the 2x4 turned out 245 hp, or 270 with the hot cam.

4. Like the '56 models, the 1957 Chevy featured a gas tank filler that was concealed behind the trim on the left rear fender.

5. Hot '57 2-doors were competitive in stock classes at the drags throughout the late '50's.

6. With their roomy interiors and large trunks, '57's are still good for daily transportation.

7. Highly sought after today as a comparatively rare collector's car, especially on the West Coast, the '57 Nomad wagon is most valuable of the mid-'50's Chevys. A classic!

7

two 12-in. shackles, you're flirting with disaster! Conversly, if the car is lowered too much, even though this can improve handling if the right springs are used, the car may prove impractical because of reduced ground clearance when entering parking lot ramps and driveways.

The best way to set up the early Chevy chassis is by parts swapping. As with early Fords, there are tremendous interchange possibilities when working with the '55-'57 Chevys. For both performance and handling, your best bet in springs is to install new ones. Let's face it, every part on your car is 15 yrs. old, and your springs and shocks probably aren't up to the task anymore. If you go the new springs route, your best bet is to get a set for a 9-passenger station wagon. The '55-'57 Chevy passenger cars used 4-leaf rear springs, with 5-leaf springs on regular station wagons, but the 9-passenger wagon introduced in '56 had 6-leaf rear springs. If you can't get new parts, then scrounge the wrecking yards for station wagon springs. And if you can't find any, you can always get two more passenger car springs and cut the eyes off the main leaves and add these shortened leaves to your own springs. Try to get new springs if you can though, as junkyard springs have probably lost their springing qualities, just like yours did. You

1. There are a lot of 2-door 210's still around. Any one of them would make a good starting point for a street 'n' stripper.

2. Jacking up the suspension like this is done for looks but usually is detrimental to safe handling on corners. We've seen some Chevys you could park a sports car under!

3. Bolt-on traction bars are good on street machines because you can leave out spring clamp for normal driving. Arrow shows clamp mount.

4. Several big, late rear ends will swap easily into the early Chevy, notably the '57-'64 Pontiac or the late 12-bolt rear from any GM car.

5. Adding new tubular front frame rails and tube axle shaves several hundred pounds from the front end.

6. If you want that jacked-up look on your street machine, you can use longer shackles in back and remove the heavy front bumper.

7. Removing the front bumper will give your front end that "ready for action" look, but then you should add some nice chrome nerf bars like these to protect the front end.

don't want the suspension *too* stiff, though.

Other chassis aids that will prove helpful include a set of traction bars to prevent rear spring wrap-up on acceleration and deceleration. There are a zillion different types and brands on the market today, ranging from large and small weld-on types to the bolt-on models that are held on by the rear spring U-bolts. The latter are the most flexible for the street, since you can remove the forward spring clamp for normal driving or clamp it up for running at the track. Parts like air bags and air shocks are OK if you don't overdo the air pressure! They shouldn't be used merely to raise the car on the street, but to put more pressure onto the right rear wheel for better traction at the drags.

While we're at the rear of the car, let's discuss rear axles for a moment. The performance enthusiast is in luck if he chooses a '55-'57 Chevy to build up, because right from the start he has a good performance axle ratio. Many guys don't know it, but the *stock* ratios on '55 and '56's were 3.55 for automatics, 3.70 for sticks, and 4.11 for overdrive models. These are all good street/strip ratios, and a darn sight better for performance than the high-ratio "smog" gears offered in new cars today. The famous Positraction limited-slip differential became an option in 1957, but the '57 ratios were raised (automatics to 3.36, sticks to 3.55, overdrive models were still at 4.11) because of the smaller, 14-in. wheels used that year.

Of course, for all-out racing you will want even lower ratios, like 4.56, 4.88 or 5.12, depending on the engine you're using. Ring and pinion sets in these and other ratios are made by Schiefer and available in most speed shops. But if you're going to be racing the car full-time, especially with a big motor, you should have something stronger than the stock differential and axles. Chevys have a bad habit of breaking axles and ring gears at the drags. A number of late rear ends from big Chevys and other cars can be made to fit under the early Chevy, but in terms of cost, durability and ease of installation, one of the best swaps is a '57 Pontiac. Pontiac and Olds both had big beefy rear ends in the '50's and the Poncho fits with a minimum of hassle. All that's required is that you switch the T-fitting for the brake lines to the left side, and relocate the spring pads! Third members from Pontiacs and Olds up to 1964 will interchange with it, also. Late GM 12-bolt Posi rear ends make for a nice installation, too.

If you're intent on building a Chevy for the junior stock classes at the drags, or an all-out gasser or modified production car, here's a tip on the '55 chassis for you weight-con-scious racers. The main frame rails in 1955 were made in two ways, the majority of them from two pieces of 3-sided channel that were slipped over one another and then welded. But some of the cars came through with frames whose rails were made from 1-piece tubing. Naturally, the 1-piece frames had no welding and were lighter. It's a small point, but something to look for when you're shopping for a body and chassis to build up a racer from.

WHAT'S UP FRONT

The front end of your early Chevy should come in for some close scrutiny. This is one place on the car where you can't afford to gamble

with old, worn-out components. The first things to check out should be the ball joints. They usually wear out after 50,000 miles, and most early Chevys have at least that much mileage. Since now you're going to the trouble of replacing them, have some good ones installed. NAPA parts stores sell replacement ball joints that are adjustable; they'll outlast the stock type because you can tighten them up in the future. There are four rubber bushings on the A-arms on each side; they're usually worn too, and easy to replace if you do it when you R&R the ball joints. A new set of these bushings will restore the "tight" feeling of a good front end. Top all this off with a realignment and you're in business.

A number of things can be done to the early Chevy front to set it up for handling or racing. There are a lot of good heavy-duty shocks on the market, including adjustable ones like the Hurst Dual-Duty units which have settings for both street and strip. These and a set of new springs will do a lot for the handling of a '55-'57.

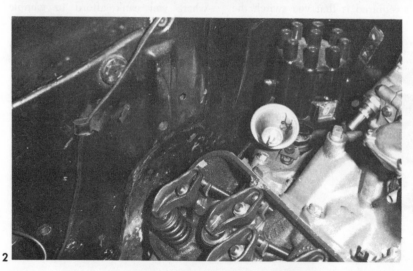

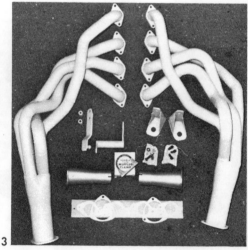

Front coil springs are some of the parts most often interchanged on these cars, as most of the later ones will fit. If you desire some heavier front springs, try the ones for a station wagon or sedan delivery; they usually have at least one more coil than your stock springs, and the later ones are thicker, too. This is the safest way to raise the Chevy's front end. If you've swapped a Rat motor into your project machine, and you're worried about the extra weight, then use coils from an air-conditioned El Camino—they'll bring that sagging nose up and then some.

There are other ways to raise the front end, but most of them are not recommended for the street. If you're really ambitious, you can cut off the front of your frame, weld on new rectangular tubing front rails and build a spring perch(es) for a tube or beam axle front end. Depending on the kind of crossmember you build and whether you use a straight or a dropped axle, this can really raise up the front end. But this is an expensive procedure that requires a lot of work, and it isn't necessary or particularly desirable for the street. You can achieve about the same thing in looks by just removing the front bumper, then you can make up some nifty little nerf bars to protect the vulnerable front sheetmetal. This shaves about 50 lbs. off the front end, too, which isn't bad. It doesn't cost you anything to do it and you can later revert back to stock with no problem.

For more front-end lift at the track under acceleration, you can get a set of ball joint spacers, called "lift kits" in the speed shop catalogs, which space the upper A-arms away from the frame and allow for more front-end rise coming off the line, which shifts weight to the rear where it's needed. When you buy a set of these spacers, make sure they are adjustable so you can realign the front end after they're installed.

In the brake department, there aren't as yet any kits made to adapt late disc brakes to the '55-'57 Chevy. For the pre-1948 Chevys, Herbert and Meek now have a kit to adapt disc binders, and for the '49-'54 kingpin-type front end there is an Airheart kit available from P.S.I. Industries, 9105 East Garvey Ave., Rosemead, Calif. 91770. One modification you *can* make to improve braking power on the '55-'57 is to adapt '59 or '60 Chevy drum front brakes, which have almost twice the area of your drums. You have to use the later parts complete with spindle and all, and it takes some adaptation, but it can be done. You have to use longer bolts on the A-arms to get the alignment right and use a tapered shim on the lower ball joint, but with these brakes and some Velvetouch metallic linings, it's almost as good as discs.

ENGINES AND TRANSMISSIONS

Now we're getting down to cases, where the true merit of the mid-'50's Chevys comes in. The sky is virtually the limit as far as engines go in the '55-'57 Chevy; every engine that Chevy made then and since then can be fitted without great difficulty. If your car was originally a V-8 model, then any of the small-block engines, from 265-283-307-327-350-400 will bolt right in just like replacing the stock engine! Thousands of these cars are out running around on the streets

1. The 396-427-454 Rat motor is a natural for the early Chevy, but tubing headers are necessary, and the firewall and clutch linkage must be reworked for swap. It makes for an instant updating in terms of power. Note that on this stock '57 the left side of the firewall need not be hammered (arrow).

2. The right side of the firewall on '55's and '56's must be pounded back to clear the Rat valve covers and heads. The left side must be reworked on all the '55-'57's.

3. A complete kit, with everything but the elbow grease is available at most speed shops for the big Rat swap. Kits can usually be purchased with or without the tube headers.

4. Ball joint spacers like these will give the front end more lift on acceleration. Make sure the ones you buy are adjustable as far as front-end alignment is concerned.

5. The ubiquitous small-block can be found, in every stage of tune, from mild to all-out, in thousands of street 'n' strip '55-'57 Chevys.

6. Adding a simple crossmember and shortening the driveshaft (depends on engine setback) will add sweet-shifting late Turbo Hydra-Matic to the early Chevy. Front driveshaft yoke from Turbo must be used also.

7. The Turbo's vacuum modulator just clears the right frame mount on Chevy. Arrow points to steel line which runs to intake manifold.

6

7

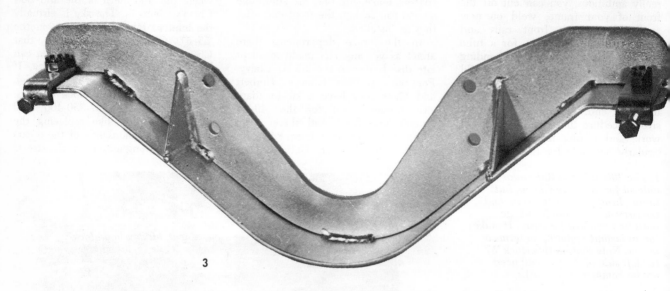

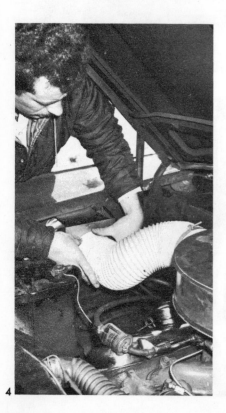

'55 to '57...

with early and late small-blocks in every conceivable state of modification. The small-block is still a cheap and easy route to performance with these cars, with the scads of new and used speed equipment available. We won't go into detail here on the limitless possibilities the small-block presents for modification; that's covered elsewhere in this book. What we're concerned with here are the swapping possibilities, and there are more than you may think.

Still talking about the small-block swaps, there are a few little hints we can pass on. The only trouble area when swapping later blocks into the early chassis is with flywheels, bellhousing and starters. Most guys try to use the late block with the early bellhousing and mounts. This is OK, but the late blocks use a starter that bolts up to the block with two vertical bolts, while the '55-'57's use a starter that bolted *back* to the *bellhousing* with *three* horizontal bolts. The solu-

1. *Using a late 3- or 4-speed stick with a late bellhousing (one that doesn't have the side mount provisions) necessitates making up some kind of rear crossmember.*

2. *The interiors of the '55-'57's are big enough so that a number of late-model front and rear seats are adaptable. This is a Camaro bench seat, with armrest, in a '56.*

3. *When using a single rear mount with Turbo or late stick, switch to a "saddle"-type front engine mount like this Hurst, or build a pair of side mounts like late cars.*

4. *The heater duct on the '57 is a natural place to install pickup for your ram-air system. After all, factory ventilation system in 1957 flowed 750 cfm at only 60 mph!*

5. *Vertical brace behind the rear seat on the early Chevy is perfect spot to mount electric fuel pump. It's close to the gas tank, but you don't have to crawl underneath the car to work on it.*

6. *A neat, hidden hood lock can be made by attaching a length of chain to the hood so that it goes through the hole in radiator splash pan. Lock goes through extra link welded to frame underneath.*

tion is to use the early starter with your early bellhousing; all you have to do is grind down one of the "ears" of the early starter to clear the late block. Grind it away to within about ⅛-inch of the top bolt-hole. Of course, if you want the advantage of the better late starter, then you have to use the late bellhousing as well, in which case everything bolts up like stock except that now you can't use the two rear mounts that bolt to the frame rails. So this requires that you make up a new rear crossmember to hold up the back of the engine/trans. A note of caution here: When switching to a single-point mounting in the rear (compared to the stock setup with two mounts in front and two in back), you may be inviting excessive engine rocking because the stock front mounts are close enough together to be almost like a single mount, in which case your engine can rock on a setup that is like one mount in front and one in back. You can get away with it if your engine is basically a stocker, but for a Rat

or a hot small-block we'd recommend switching to a wide-stance front mount like a Hurst, or building mounts off the sides of the block like the later cars.

Like the old saying goes, "You can't beat cubic inches." The early Chevy engineers must have had this thought in the back of their minds when they designed the '55-'57's, because the big Rat fits in with comparative ease. The main thing about this swap is that a set of tubing headers are required, in order to clear the steering and other components, because the stock manifolds won't fit. This isn't such a bad thing, because most of you would want to add a set of headers, anyway. Other changes include modifying the clutch linkage and hammering back the firewall to clear the back of the heads. The 1957 models already have a depression in the firewall on the right side, but on '55 and '56's you'll have to hit both sides. The easiest way is to use a sledgehammer on the firewall, with the engine out of the car, after

you've tried the engine for fit to see where the interference is. Carefully done and painted over after the hammering, it's hard to tell that the firewall had to be whacked.

The Rat motor is one case where we would not recommend using the stock-type front mounts, but rather the wide-stance front mount or side mounts. That's an elephant-killer load of low-end torque you're adding there and you don't want it rocking back and forth in the frame! The whole kaboodle for the Rat swap is available in kit form from: Hurst Performance, Inc., 50 West St., Warminster, Pa. 18974; and Herbert & Meek, 11121 Magnolia Blvd., No. Hollywood, Calif. 91601. They can set you up with all the parts and pieces, even headers, and most of the big header companies have headers to fit such a swap. The Rat adds about 90 lbs. to your front end compared to the small-block, which is not a great deal but enough to make your tired front springs really start to sag. The solution is a new set of springs, like late-

1

2

3

'55 to '57...

model El Camino coils, to bring the front end back up. All in all, swapping the Rat into the early Chevy is a highly satisfying project, with plenty of street/strip and freeway power, and the torque to pull stumps or tow a trailer with a race car.

Late transmissions are swapped into these cars even more easily than the late engines are. The 3-speeds, 4-speeds and Turbo Hydra-Matics are easily installed, and the natural complement of an engine swap. With late 3-speeds, which are shorter than the mid-'50's Chevys. You have to lengthen your driveshaft some, but late BW T-10 and Muncie 4-speeds are the same length as the early 3-speed. The rugged, good-shifting Turbo Hydro makes a great addition to the mid-'50's Chevys. You have to mount a new crossmember between

1. The 283-hp 283 engine, with Rochester fuel injection, was the hottest thing going in 1957; still holds its own in the lower NHRA "junior stock" classes.

2. In both the stock and hot classes, the station wagon remains popular due to its weight transfer.

3. The "economy" route to wider wheels for your Chevy is a set of Corvette rims. These are 8 ins. wide yet fit under stock fenderwell. These wheels will not fit front hubs unless you enlarge center hole a little with a file.

4. Although later cars like the Camaros, Corvettes and MoPars are taking over the upper classes, the '55-'57 is still a good machine for the lower gas and M/P classes.

5. With a strong, light chassis, easily set up with traction bars, lift kits, etc., the '55-'57 Chevy has become the '32 Ford of the '60's. Since the recent advent of supercar insurance hassles, you can expect to see more and more of these cars built to high-performance specs for street and strip use.

need to use a Rat starter motor. This also gives additional starting power, which is something to consider if you have a lot of compression in your engine. We would recommend the 350 Turbo as good for most small-block applications, but for a 396-427-454 Rat or even a hot small-block, the beefier 400 is the way to go. In either case, if your early Chevy was a stick before you swapped, you'll also have to change your radiator for an automatic type which has the bottom tank and fittings for the automatic's cooling lines.

The mid-'50's Chevys are still available in reasonably sound condition for a good price (unless you're after a Nomad), and they present the average rodder with an opportunity to build a practical street/strip performer by getting the most for his money. And with the way drag racing has been changing, what with the early cars being phased out of the junior stock ranks and the modified production classes being now dominated by later cars, we can probably look forward to seeing a lot of sharp race cars converted back to yeoman duty on the street. We say, "Long live the '55-'57, the best Chevys ever built!"

the frame rails to hold the transmission, and depending on the engine setback involved, you may have to shorten your driveshaft an inch or so. A Hurst Auto-Stick or Dual-Gate shifter will handle the gear selection and both offer two sets of stick detents to operate normally or shift manually. The only other modification is to add a Turbo Hydro driveshaft front yoke to your shaft, because the Turbo has a different output spline. When using a 400-type Turbo with a small-block motor, you'll and 283 cubic inches. The other two power plants available are the Turbo-Fire 265 V-8, listing 265 inches, eight to one compression and a single two-barrel carburetor; and the Blue-Flame Six, boosted this year to 235 inches with eight to one compression and single barrel carburetion. A selection of four transmissions also are listed, including the new Turboglide, Power-glide, Overdrive and the standard Syn-chro-Mesh with a clutch. The test car was equipped with Powerglide and the Super Turbo-Fire V-8 engine with a single four-barrel.

In the engine department, I think someone missed the boat when they stuck an air cleaner on those big car-buretors without allowing for more air intake. The air cleaner takes in air through a small tunnel-like opening in the front which doesn't seem big enough to take in any great quantity of air to the carburetor. However, the engineers did a bang up job on the design of the power brake reserve tank located under the hood. It is made of metal, pressed together in two parts and then welded like a gas tank.

Driving the new Chevy was pretty pleasant duty. It rode well, handled well, performed well. The test started at the Southern California Auto Club, where we had the speedometer and odometer checked for error and correc-tion which we used later in our ac-celeration runs. Most of the actual testing was done on a comparatively new road racing course at the Para-mount Ranch near Agura, California. But one of the best tests of all came on the return trip through Los Angeles during the rush hour.

My first impression of the car, after getting on the road, centered around the transmission. As mentioned the test car was equipped with Powerglide but, contrary to other Chevrolets I've driven, this one seemed to have a more direct drive with less slippage than I expected. The new Turboglide transmission also is available this year with a hill retarder gear that helps brake the car on steep inclines. An auto-matic transmission with three turbines doing the work, it's new this year, and was designed for a smoother, unbroken flow of power on take-off.

Since the car was equipped with power steering and brakes, we put them to test by shutting off the power while still in motion. There was a noticeable difference in the steering with power off, but nothing to bring on a wrassle with the steering wheel. And the brakes worked perfectly, despite the lack of power, which is nice to know in case

of an emergency.

On the open highway, I put the car into some tight turns at 60 mph, and there was the slightest indication of front end dive, noticeable only under hard cornering conditions. Otherwise, it handled well in the turns with the exception of shocks. They could have been heavier to improve handling.

On the test course, I was able to corner a bit harder for a more com-plete test of handling. There was con-siderable lean but I didn't experience any rocking motion through the turns. I think heavier shocks would have pre-vented the dipping and made it pos-sible to get into the corners harder.

Steering was not oversensitive. I thought it felt very stable for a power unit. Cornering, I could feel a slight road pull which I think is best anyway, and yet the power made it easy. I got into one turn a little too hot and had to correct in a hurry but when I did, the car recovered quickly and I never lost the feel of the front end at all.

Good seating and visibility had a lot to do with how the car felt for handling. You sit rather high in the car, giving a clear view of the road and front of the car. It helps give you a command of the machine and road as well, and I think that's important in any automobile and should be con-sidered when testing for handling.

The ride itself, both on the highway and on the race course, was not uncom-fortable. The suspension was firm, han-dling the bumps and dips nicely, and still it was comfortable. Chevrolet has an all steel body this year, with double walled doors and a roof bow that acts something like a roll bar in emergen-cies. I couldn't find any vibrations or loose rattles in the body.

As for acceleration, the engine packed plenty of punch. Only in one case did I find any hesitation, and that was in shifting the gear selector from low to drive range under acceleration. There was a noticeable split-second hesitation there before the rpm con-tinued upward. We wound the engine pretty tight, even in low range, but there was no valve chatter or excessive vibration despite this heavy abuse. The engine itself still was tight, but in all of our test runs, the temperature remained normal.

Our acceleration runs were ham-pered slightly by a strong wind, but we made several checks in all speed ranges to give us an accurate reading. Here are the results:

0-60	9.3 sec.
0-50	7.0 sec.
0-40	5.2 sec.
0-30	4.0 sec.

The top speed run was bothered also by the strong wind, and the engine probably would have put out a bit more

top end punch had there been a few more miles on it. However, we came up with a reading of 111.3 mph which is not at all unimpressive.

After our acceleration runs, which called for plenty of stop-and-go driv-ing and exercise of the brakes, I found considerable brake fade. They re-covered but not too quickly. However, when they did recover, I could still bring the car to an even stop without the brakes pulling to one side.

As mentioned, the return trip from the road course was a test in itself, as only driving in downtown and Free-way traffic around Los Angeles can be. It was a good opportunity to feel the car out for ease of handling in tight squeezes, for those rush hours can be worse than the first lap of a stock car race on a quarter-mile race track.

I found that I could work the car through traffic without getting into tight squeezes. The power steering helped in maneuvering, and a good punch from the engine made it easy to outrun heavy traffic leaving a sig-nal. And another feature that I liked was the brake pedal. I don't brake with my left foot, even in a race car, but I move it around a lot while I'm driv-ing. The Chevy's pedal is wide but not so wide as to interfere with my foot movement.

Like most '57 automobiles, Chev-rolet has gone for the new 7.50 x 14 tires which do have their advantages. However, I would like to see Chevro-lets use a padded dash like many of the new cars. It not only is a safety fea-ture but helps eliminate glare during bright sunlight.

Too, I believe an improvement could be made in the action of the special passing or kick-down gear which cuts in with a punch of the throttle and gives you a boost when you might need it. This passing gear cuts in at speeds of 48 mph or under, and cuts out at about 58 mph. Since much of your passing is done on the open highway at speeds above 48 mph, this isn't too practical. It would help a great deal if it were set to kick in at speeds up to at least 55 mph.

In conclusion, I do feel that Chev-rolet, and many other futuristic minded manufacturers have learned a great deal from stock car racing throughout the country, and have put their knowl-edge to good use. The sport has proved many ideas and disproved many others, while the automobile world has bene-fited.

The same holds true for Indian-apolis, home of the annual 500-mile race, world's greatest sports event for my money and a top proving ground for future engineering designs and ideas. Indianapolis and big time racing are responsible for many of the plea-sures enjoyed in passenger cars. ●